FRSAD

FRSAD
Conceptual Modeling of Aboutness

MAJA ŽUMER, MARCIA LEI ZENG, AND ATHENA SALABA

Third Millennium Cataloging
SUSAN LAZINGER AND SHEILA INTNER, SERIES EDITORS

AN IMPRINT OF ABC-CLIO, LLC
Santa Barbara, California • Denver, Colorado • Oxford, England

Library of Congress Cataloging-in-Publication Data

Žumer, Maja.
 FRSAD : conceptual modeling of aboutness / Maja Žumer, Marcia Lei Zeng, and Athena Salaba.
  pages cm. — (Third millennium cataloging)
 Includes bibliographical references and index.
  ISBN 978–1–59884–794–9 (pbk.) — ISBN 978–1–59884–795–6 (ebook) (print)
1. FRSAD (Conceptual model) 2. Subject headings. I. Zeng, Marcia Lei, 1956– II. Salaba, Athena.
III. Title.
Z666.63.F77Z86   2012
025.4′7—dc23   2012016610

ISBN: 978–1–59884–794–9
EISBN: 978–1–59884–795–6

16 15 14 13 12   1 2 3 4 5

This book is also available on the World Wide Web as an eBook.
Visit www.abc-clio.com for details.

Libraries Unlimited
An Imprint of ABC-CLIO, LLC

ABC-CLIO, LLC
130 Cremona Drive, P.O. Box 1911
Santa Barbara, California 93116-1911

This book is printed on acid-free paper ∞

Manufactured in the United States of America

Contents

CHAPTER 1

Introduction

The International Federation of Library Associations and Institutions (IFLA) has been involved in the development of a number of standards for metadata creation and models of the bibliographic universe. In 1998, IFLA published the *Functional Requirements for Bibliographic Records* (FRBR), an entity-relationship conceptual model of bibliographic data approved by IFLA in 1997 and prepared by the FRBR Working Group. The group's objectives were to "provide a clearly defined, structured framework for relating the data that are recorded in bibliographic records to the needs of the users of those records" and "to recommend a basic level of functionality for records created by national bibliographic agencies" (FRBR, 1998, p. 7). The published FRBR report identifies, names, and defines the entities used in the model to represent the bibliographic universe, the attributes associated with each entity, and the primary relationships that exist among entities and, in some cases, between specific instances of entities. Finally, in order to show the functional requirements, it maps the attributes to the four general user tasks defined in the report. A total of 10 entities were originally defined (*work, expression, manifestation, item, person, corporate body, concept, object, event,* and *place*) grouped in three entity groups. The entity *family* was added to Group 2 entities later as part of *Functional Requirements for Authority Data* (FRAD). Table 1.1 lists the entities and user tasks identified and defined in the FRBR models.

TABLE 1.1   Overview of FRBR, FRAD, and FRSAD

FRBR	FRAD	FRSAD
	ENTITIES	
Group 1	Work	*Thema*
Work	Expression	*Nomen*
Expression	Manifestation	
Manifestation	Item	
Item	Person	
Group 2	Corporate Body	
Person	*Family*	
Corporate Body	Concept	
Group 3	Object	
Concept	Event	
Object	Place	

(continued)

TABLE 1.1 (Continued)

FRBR	FRAD	FRSAD
	ENTITIES	
Event Place	*Name* *Identifier* *Controlled Access Point* *Rules* *Agency*	
	USER TASKS	
Find one Group 1 entity or entities	**Find** one entity or entities	**Find** a subject entity or entities
Identify one Group 1 entity or entities	**Identify** one entity or entities	**Identify** a subject entity or entities
Select one Group 1 entity or entities		**Select** a subject entity or entities
Obtain one Group 1 entity or entities		
	Contextualize, place in context, explore relationships	
		Explore relationships and domains
	Justify the form of an access point	

Since the FRBR model placed a main focus on the bibliographic data, an additional group, the Functional Requirements and Numbering of Authority Records (FRANAR) Working Group, was established "to provide a framework for the analysis of functional requirements for the kind of authority data that is required to support authority control and for the international sharing of authority data" (FRAD, 2009, p. 13). In its effort to model authority data associated with *works* and Group 2 entities, the group identified and defined additional entities in the FRAD. These entities include *family*, *name*, *identifier*, *controlled access point*, *rules*, and *agency*. In the same tradition as the FRBR model, FRAD defined the general user tasks for authority data and inherent relationships between entities.

Even though FRAD covers authority data, the main focus was on Group 2 entities. A third IFLA working group, the Functional Requirements for Subject Authority Records (FRSAR) Working Group, was established in 2005, before the publication of FRAD in 2010, to provide "a clearly stated and commonly shared understanding of what the subject authority data/record/file aims to provide information about, and the expectation of what such data should achieve in terms of answering user needs" (FRSAD, 2011, p. 6). The focus of the *Functional*

Requirements for Subject Authority Data (FRSAD) report is to model the entities as they relate to the aboutness of a work. FRSAD identified and defined two new high-level entities for subject authority data, *thema* and *nomen*, and relationships between *themas*, between *thema* and *nomen*, and between *nomens*. User tasks as they relate to the use of subject authority data are also defined. Table 1.1 lists the entities and user tasks identified and defined in the FRAD model as they compare to the FRBR model. Entities in italics indicate added entities.

At the time of writing the IFLA FRBR Review Group will harmonize the three models as one FRBR family model in order to solve some issues resulting from differences in the modeling approaches, such as varied definitions of entities and differences in attributes. The harmonized model will therefore provide one unified model for implementation.

This book is based on the FRSAD model, which is a collective intellectual work of the IFLA FRSAR Working Group. It enables the authors to give an overview of modeling of aboutness in general and to compare FRSAD with other models that have emerged recently, as well as demonstrate its applicability for future implementations. It is written for any library and information professional who wants to have a better understanding of FRSAD and its relationship to the other two FRBR family models. It is also meant as a guide for knowledge organization system (KOS) developers who may want to apply the FRSAD model to their subject authority data.

The book is arranged in three parts. The first part (Chapters 1–3) provides the background analysis that led to the development of the FRSAD model. Chapter 1, "Introduction," places the development of the FRSAD model in the context of the FRBR family models. Chapter 2, "Aboutness," offers a general discussion on aboutness and compares the concepts of *aboutness*, *ofness*, and *isness*, necessary discussions that will help the reader understand the scope of the FRSAD model and this book. Chapter 3, "Users and Use of Subject Authority Data," covers the different user groups and their uses of subject authority data, tying this discussion to the FRSAD user tasks and providing a number of use scenarios as illustrations.

The second part (Chapters 4 and 5) describes the model and its components including entities, relationships between different entities and between the instances of the same entity, and all entity attributes. Chapter 4, "Modeling Approaches," offers a number of approaches for modeling the "has subject" relationship. The approaches include those proposed by FRBR, FRAD, FRSAD, <indecs>, Ranganathan, Dahlberg, Buizza and Guerrini, and FAST. Chapter 5, "The FRSAD Model," describes in detail the model and provides examples to illustrate the different components of the model.

The third part (Chapters 6–8) presents subject authority data units of existing common vocabularies through the FRSAD model. Significant issues of interoperability related to data models, KOS structures, and applications are summarized in the last chapter. Chapter 6, "Formal Presentations of the FRSAD Model," presents different formal presentations of FRSAD for implementation, including a summary of the model, expressed in the Resource Description Framework (RDF). Chapter 7, "Examples of Subject Authority Systems Explained Using the FRSAD Model," offers examples of existing subject authority systems and illustrates how they can be explained using the FRSAD model. Chapter 8, "Use of FRSAD Model for KOS Development and Interoperability," explains different scenarios for KOS development, implications for community-specific vocabularies, vocabulary mapping, and data modeling for interoperability.

REFERENCES

Functional Requirements for Authority Data: A Conceptual Model (FRAD). (2009). IFLA Working Group on Functional Requirements and Numbering of Authority Records (FRANAR). Ed. Glenn E. Patton. München: K.G. Saur.

Functional Requirements for Bibliographic Records: Final Report (FRBR). (1998). IFLA Study Group on the Functional Requirements for Bibliographic Records. München: K.G. Saur. Available at http://www.ifla.org/files/cataloguing/frbr/frbr.pdf (accessed January 20, 2010).

Functional Requirements for Subject Authority Data: A Conceptual Model (FRSAD). (2011). IFLA Working Group on Functional Requirements for Subject Authority Records (FRSAR). Eds. M. L. Zeng, M. Žumer, and A. Salaba. Berlin/München: De Gruyter Saur.

CHAPTER 2

Aboutness

ABOUTNESS: OVERVIEW

Searching on a topic, also referred to as subject searching, has always been an important requirement of users of bibliographic information systems in addition to known-item searching, which is usually based on descriptive elements. When modeling the bibliographic universe, it is therefore essential to include the modeling of aboutness, the relationship between a resource and its subject matter.

Aboutness is a statement of what a work (an information resource) is about, what topics it covers. It is usually expressed with the relationship "work is about/covers/has subject x, y, and z." Information professionals, when analyzing the content of a resource through the process of identifying the topics discussed or otherwise represented in the resource, are trying to assess the user information needs that can be fulfilled by the resource at a future time. The user, on the other hand, when trying to fulfill an information need, wants to find the appropriate resources or verify whether the resource(s) obtained contain relevant information.

Both theoretical and practical approaches to the issues of subject analysis and aboutness can be found in current literature. The theoretical approach focuses on the philosophical aspects of the subject relationship, while the practical approach centers on the process of providing subject access in bibliographic information systems and its use. Patrick Wilson has included a philosophical analysis of aboutness in a chapter, "Subjects and the Sense of Position," in his *Two Kinds of Power* (Wilson, 1968, pp. 69–92). Wilson compares works or writings with physical objects and discusses some of the differences in subject analysis. The subjects of works are not easy to determine, and it is not always possible to come up with the same subject term or the correct one when considering two equally specific or equally exhaustive subject statements, unlike the shapes or sizes of physical objects, which are more easily or consistently identified. This is because works do not inherently "have" subjects like physical objects have shapes. Based on Hjørland (1992), aboutness is a relation between sets of works, subjects, agents, and dates and cannot be considered as a property of works. It is not possible to objectively determine the truth in the statement "Document d is about subject z."

According to Fairthorne (1969), who takes more of a pragmatic and less of a philosophical view, it is difficult to identify which of the things that are explicitly stated in a resource refer to a relevant topic and how to identify and deal with topics that are not explicitly mentioned. In other words, the fact that some things are mentioned in a resource does not mean that the resource is about them. The metadata creators usually determine the overall topic(s) and then represent them using terms from one or more vocabularies. These processes are described as conceptual analysis and translation by Lancaster (1998). But even this process is not always straightforward because there are different ways to understand aboutness. Often, what an information professional decides a resource is about, and what a vocabulary allows him or her to express, does not coincide with what a searcher of information is expecting or is concerned with (Swift et al., 1978).

It should also be noted that even though the importance of subject indexing is well documented and understood, it has mostly been studied and implemented in the context of scholarly publications and nonfiction. It is only in recent years that this important process and the way for the user to access information has been applied to fiction and other imaginative materials (such as feature films), especially when it comes to the traditional library subject cataloging practice (see also the discussion in the next section).

The FRSAD model looks at aboutness from the users' point of view. While it may be impossible to objectively determine the topic(s) of each particular work, the users want to find resources about the topic they are interested in. When users are confronted with an information need about a certain subject, they expect to be able to structure a subject search query and expect that the tools and services available to them will effectively compare and match such search queries with the subject representations provided by metadata creators. In this way the catalog is fulfilling Cutter's (1904) second objective of enabling the user to see what the library has by an author, **on a subject**, and in a given kind of literature.

ABOUTNESS AND OFNESS

The discussion of the differences between aboutness and ofness becomes relevant when the question of "what is the subject/topic discussed or otherwise represented in this work" applies to a less- or nonsubstantive work (Lancaster, 2003, p. 200) such as a fiction, a play, a music, an image, or a film. What is a fiction "about"? Is it the message intended by the creator or the reflection of this message in the mind of a reader, observer, or listener? Is it the plot or the ideas behind it? Any work can be described in a variety of ways, from general categorization to specific indexing. The open-ended scopes of imaginative works make the analyses of their aboutness more challenging. The possibility exists that the message an imaginative work tries to deliver would be received and interpreted in various different ways by readers, observers, and listeners.

If one takes into account that a large portion of a public library's collection is fiction and usually more than half of the circulation is fictional works, it is interesting that libraries, for many years, have not considered it important to allow for subject access to fiction (Pejtersen, 1979). We know from our users that they do want to find imaginative works in a particular setting, discussing certain characters, topical areas, and so forth.

In reality, the notion of identifying the topics and providing subject access to imaginative works is perhaps skewed. Taking an example used by Lancaster (2003, p. 201) and putting it into a real title, if a user searches the term *farming* to find the 1965 film *War and Peace*, it is not because the film is about farming but because it contains some themes that have a farming setting. This is true for fiction as well. The access provided to imaginative works is often less concerned with revealing what information a work conveys (aboutness) than indicating what it depicts (ofness). It appears that regardless of the expressiveness or imaginative quality of an imaginative work, it is treated as more of documentary evidence.

Just like what was characterized by Shatford Layne (1994) on images, different kinds of information-bearing resources may convey information or meaning in ways that are inherently different from those of others. She suggested that not only do images convey information in different ways from text but they may possibly convey different information. While focusing on still images, she summarized four categories of attributes of an image or set of images: "biographical," subject, exemplified, and relationship. The first aspect of the subject attributes of images is that an image may be both *about* and *of* (Shatford Layne, 1994, p. 584), while the interpretation of the aboutness may reach a very different level. *The Last Supper* by Leonardo da Vinci certainly clearly represents a scene that many would recognize. The aboutness, with an understanding of the context in which the picture was created, would be what it symbolizes to a viewer (Svenonius, 1994). This painting is also *of* the things it represents: Jesus and his Twelve Apostles. Representational (figurative) work like this is narrative, meaning that it tells a story or represents an episode in a story (Baca et al., 2006, p. 207). Many works of art were designed or intended as allegories or symbolic expressions. Thus their aboutness can be seen as an essential element of their subject analysis (Shatford Layne, 2002). This kind of subject analysis can also presumably be applied to Rembrandt's *The Night Watch* and Michelangelo's *Pietà*. While Edvard Munch's *Scream* or Van Gogh's *The Starry Night* may be still explainable in terms of the meaning, many artworks, however, are not. The aboutness of various works of art may be more tenuous, less clear, and perhaps even an unnecessary element of subject analysis (Shatford Layne, 2002).

Many representational works, though figurative, may be nonnarrative, representing things (persons, animals, plants, buildings, or objects) depicted in a picture. Harpring (2002) listed a wide range of examples where the subject matter does not tell a story; for example, for a painting or sculpture of a genre scene, such as a young woman bathing; for a portrait, the subject can be a named sitter; for a pot, its geometric decoration or its function, and so on.

At a certain point, the abstract and subjective nature of interpreting what an imaginative or a representational work is *about* makes the attempt not only challenging but also problematic. On the contrary, what such a work is *of* tends to be more concrete and objective.

While ofness is different from aboutness, there is obviously some overlap. "In a scholarly discussion of subject matter, various areas of subject analysis are often woven together into a seamless whole" (Harpring, 2002, p. 22). When looking for information about a person, for instance Albert Einstein, one may also be interested in his portraits; when searching for information about the famous Cologne cathedral, pictures depicting the cathedral would definitely be relevant as well. In order to provide such access, libraries have traditionally included this aspect in subject access. Visual resources and museums have recommended three levels of subject analysis for works of art:

1. **Description**. Terms for description refer to generic elements depicted in or by the work. These are terms reflecting only what you would see in the subject if you did not know the specific people, event, story, or place depicted (e.g., human female, nude, column, train, etc.)

2. **Identification**. Terms for identification refer to the specific subject, including named historical, mythological, religious, fictional, or literary subjects (e.g., Hercules and Antaeus, Washington Crossing the Delaware, Battle of Waterloo, etc.)

3. **Interpretation**. Terms for interpretation refer to the meaning or themes represented by the subjects and includes a conceptual analysis of what the work is about (e.g., salvation, original sin, sacrifice, truth, power, innocence, idolatry) (Baca and Harpring, 2009, Section 16.)

FORM, GENRE, AND ISNESS

Nonrepresentational works also exist in many formats. An instance of architecture, decoration, or furniture may have no narrative or figurative subject matter. When they also need to be described, documented, and accessed, the important attributes may be their function, form or composition, style, and genre (Baca et al., 2006, p. 207).

With these kinds of needs in mind, information professionals also describe or document other aspects of intellectual and artistic works in addition to their aboutness and ofness, such as form, genre, and targeted audience. For example:

- An electronic resource (format) about teaching reading skills (aboutness)
- A sound recording (format) of piano music (genre)
- A flash card (format) game (genre) for learning addition (aboutness) for preschool children (audience)
- A digital file (format) of a landscape photograph (genre) of the Grand Canyon (ofness)

Form and genre are considered as aspects of *isness* because they imply what class a work belongs to according to its attributes—for instance, it is a novel versus a poem; it is a concerto versus a sonata; it is an architectural drawing of a building versus a photograph of a building. All these imply of what type a work *is* rather than what a work is *about*. In the FRBR model, some of these properties are already modeled as *work* attributes, for example, "form of work" and "intended audience." The discussion here for *isness* should not be confused with works that are written *about* a form or genre, for instance, about romance novels, about documentary films, or about photographs.

THE COMMON NEEDS THAT STRUCTURED VOCABULARIES SERVE

It is beyond the scope of this book to address aboutness of works in specific fields of humanities such as literary criticism, musicology, or history of art. However, this does not mean that the model for aboutness cannot be applied to ofness or beyond when the appellations of a thing need to be controlled. Obviously, in the traditional sense, the KOS are created to facilitate the description of the aboutness. Many KOS such as subject-heading schemes, thesauri, and classification systems were developed to respond to the need of library and information professionals to describe and organize bibliographic materials. More and more systems have also been adopted to describe and organize nonbibliographic materials, for example, the surrogates of works of arts and architecture in slide libraries, photographic archives, and repositories. In addition, KOS have found perfect use cases in describing, documenting, and providing access to the objects themselves in the case of museums, archives, galleries, inventories, and repositories (Baca, 2004). Although subject authority data have been used for various functions and reasons, they have been used to address not only the aboutness but also ofness and isness of works in various domains. There are obvious common needs for structured vocabularies.

REFERENCES

Baca, Murtha. (2004). Fear of Authority? Authority Control and Thesaurus Building for Art and Material Culture Information. *Cataloging & Classification Quarterly* 38 (3&4): 143–51.

Baca, Murtha, et al., eds. (2006). *Cataloging Cultural Objects: A Guide to Describing Cultural Works and Their Images.* Chicago: American Library Association.

Baca, Murtha, and Patricia Harpring, eds. (2009 rev.). *Categories for the Description of Works of Art.* The Getty Research Institute. Online version: http:// www.getty.edu/research/publications/electronic_publications/cdwa/index .html.

Cutter, Charles Ami. (1904). *Rules for a Printed Dictionary Catalogue.* 4th ed. Washington: Government Printing Office.

Fairthorne, R. A. (1969). "Content Analysis, Specification and Control." *Annual Review of Information Science and Technology* 4, 71–109.

Goodman, Nelson. (1961). "About." *Mind* 70 (277): 1–24.

Harpring, Patricia. (2002). "The Language of Images: Enhancing Access to Images by Applying Metadata Schemas and Structured Vocabularies." In *Introduction to Art Image Access: Issues, Tools, Standards, and Strategies*, edited by Murtha Baca, pp. 1–19. Los Angeles: Getty Research Institute.

Hjørland, Birger. (1992). "The Concept of 'Subject' in Information Science." *Journal of Documentation* 48 (2): 172–200.

Lancaster, F. W. (1998). *Indexing and Abstracting in Theory and Practice*, 2nd ed. Champaign: University of Illinois.

Lancaster, F. W. (2003). *Indexing and Abstracting in Theory and Practice*, 3rd ed. Champaign: University of Illinois.

Pejtersen, A. M. (1979). "The Meaning of 'About' in Fiction Indexing and Retrieval. *Aslib Proceedings* 31, 251–57.

Shatford Layne, S. (1994). "Some Issues in the Indexing of Images." *Journal of the American Society for Information Science* 45 (8): 583–88.

Shatford Layne, S. (2002). "Subject Access to Art Images." In *Introduction to Art Image Access: Issues, Tools, Standards, and Strategies*, edited by Murtha Baca, pp. 1–19. Los Angeles: Getty Research Institute.

Svenonius, E. (1994). "Access to Nonboom Materials: The Limits of Subject Indexing for Visual and Aural Languages." *Journal of the American Society for Information Science* 45 (8): 600–606.

Swift, D. E., et al. (1978). " 'Aboutness' as a Strategy for Retrieval in the Social Sciences." *Aslib Proceedings* 30, 182–87.

Wilson, Patrick. (1968). *Two Kinds of Power: An Essay on Bibliographic Control*. Berkeley: University of California Press.

CHAPTER 3

Users and Use of Subject Authority Data

WHO ARE THE USERS OF SUBJECT AUTHORITY DATA?

When discussing conceptual modeling of subject authority data, it is essential to analyze who the users of these data are, to identify contexts of the use of the data, and to describe some of the use scenarios. The identification of the types of users and how they use the data determines what the necessary attributes and relationships are to support different user tasks.

While usually not designed for end users or directly accessible to end users, authority data should be considered a valuable information resource and made available to users for browsing or searching. Such direct use of authority data would fulfill, for example, the need for getting acquainted with the terminology and exploring a subject domain. On the other hand, authority data are often used indirectly in the process of creating bibliographic data or as a means to search and find bibliographic data. Possible subject authority data user groups include: (a) information professionals who create metadata; (b) controlled vocabulary creators, such as catalogers or thesaurus and ontology creators; (c) reference and public services librarians and other information professionals who are searching for information as intermediaries; (d) end users using information retrieval systems to fulfill their information needs; and (e) machines harvesting subject authority data and linking data. Two of these user types, intermediaries (c) and end users (d), can be grouped together as users who use subject authority data to search for bibliographic data. Metadata creators (a) use subject authority data directly and indirectly though bibliographic data. Vocabulary creators (b) use subject data directly. Information intermediaries (c) and end users (d) most often use these data indirectly via the interface that allows them access to bibliographic data. Machines (e) may use the subject authority data directly or indirectly via bibliographic data. Figure 3.1 displays the four-point perspective of subject authority data users.

A discussion of how each group uses subject authority data follows based on existing literature and the findings of two surveys conducted by the FRSAR Working Group.

FIGURE 3.1   Subject authority data users.

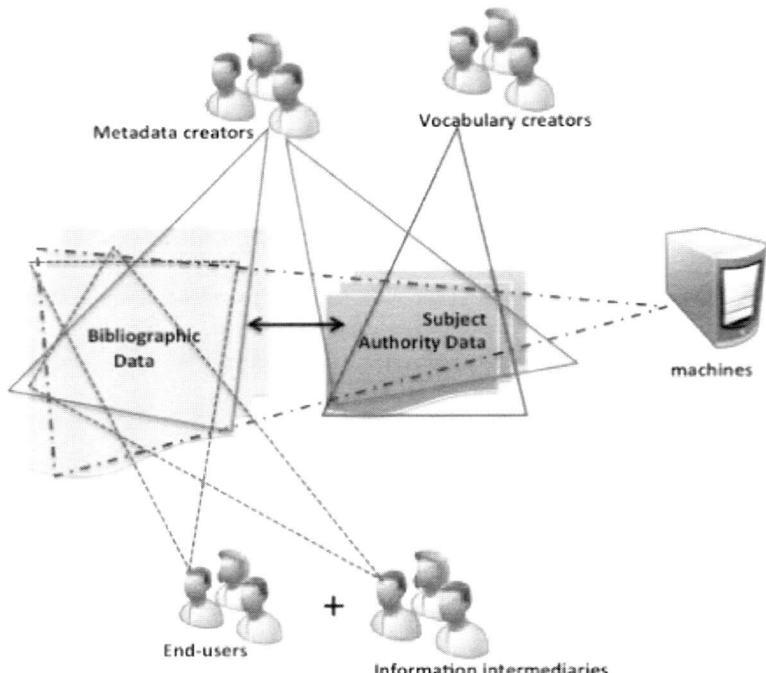

USER STUDIES AND THEIR USE OF SUBJECT AUTHORITY DATA

A number of studies have examined the use of subject authority data by different user groups. From the literature we see that the major focus of user studies is the users who use subject authority data indirectly as a means to find information stored as bibliographic data. A few studies examining the information-seeking behavior of information professionals tended to also study the use of subject authority data from the searching aspect. Catalog-use studies are the majority of research studies that discuss users of subject data. These include academic library users (e.g., Hunter, 1991; Peters and Kurth, 1991; Wilkes and Nelson, 1995; Yu and Young, 2004; Liu, 2009); some general users, often experts and novice users; domain experts; and information professionals (Alpi, 2005).

At the initial stage of the development of the FRSAD model, the FRSAR Working Group felt strongly that, in order to define user tasks, an actual user study was necessary. Two studies were therefore conducted. The first was a pilot study at the 2006 Semantic Technologies Conference (San Jose, California, USA). Most of the participants of this first study were either creators of semantic tools, including controlled vocabularies, taxonomies, and ontologies, or developers and managers of semantic technology systems (this study will be referred to as the "semantic survey" henceforth). Participants were asked to describe their work and in what ways they use semantic tool data. For the second study, an international survey was sent to information professionals

FIGURE 3.2   Subject authority data users and their work.

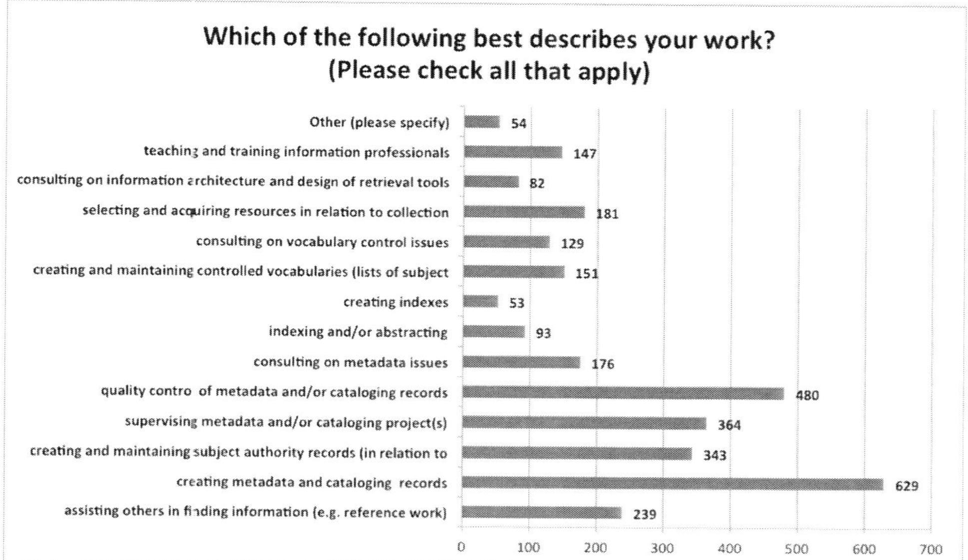

throughout the world during the months of May through September 2006 (the study will be referred to as the "international survey" henceforth). Participants included authority record creators, vocabulary creators and managers, catalogers, metadata librarians, and reference librarians, among others. Participants were asked to describe their work and their use of subject authority data in different contexts, including cataloging and metadata creation, subject authority work, and searching or helping others search bibliographic information.

The largest group from the 798 participants of the international study represented professionals working in the creation of metadata and cataloging records (78.8%). Others were involved with quality control or supervision of metadata and cataloging processes and projects, creation of controlled vocabularies and other KOS, and about 30% of all participants assisted others in finding information (reference work). Figure 3.2 offers details of participant responses when asked to describe their work.

Use of subject authority data findings from both the semantic and international studies are reported in this chapter as they apply under each type of group.

USE OF SUBJECT AUTHORITY DATA BY VOCABULARY CREATORS

Best practice for developing and maintaining subject authority data and other vocabulary information should follow international standards such as ISO 2788. The process of creating and maintaining subject authority data involves finding all the terms that represent a concept, often selecting one to serve as the preferred term, linking to terms representing other semantically related concepts, updating the vocabulary, and consulting and citing sources.

FIGURE 3.3   Use of subject authority data by semantic participants.

In what ways do you use the semantic tools? (Ranked according the number of answers)
To explore a topic through browsing synonymous and related terms
other:
—To discover relationships.
— For systems engineering.
—Software development.
—Data integration/system engineering.
—Creating tools to process and use ontologies for data integration.
—Research.
—Software development.
—Training others on semantic tools.
—Moving from doc-oriented technical publications to topic-based (i.e., DITA) technical documentation.
—Semantic web development tools.
—Service ontologies.
—Combine three kinds of semantics.

Figure 3.3 provides a summary of participant responses from the semantic survey when they were asked how they use subject authority data.

In the international survey, among the participants who use subject authority data in subject authority work, a majority use the data to normalize and standardize terms. They also modify authority data, maintain data for future use, and establish and update term relationships (Figure 3.4).

FIGURE 3.4   Use of subject authority data in subject authority work.

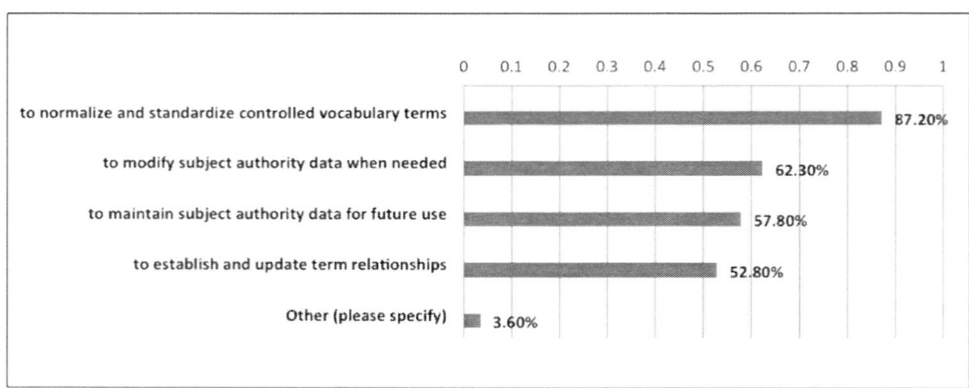

Both surveys show that information professionals who create and maintain subject authority data perform tasks such as standardization of the vocabulary that represents subject concepts; discovering, establishing, and updating relationships; becoming familiar with a domain's vocabulary; and developing semantic tools.

USE OF SUBJECT AUTHORITY DATA AT THE CREATION AND MAINTENANCE OF DATA: METADATA CREATORS

Part of the process of metadata creation is the process of assigning subjects and classification numbers to metadata records. In this process, metadata creators consult subject authority data to ensure that the most appropriate valid subjects are assigned. In addition, changes made to the subject authority data have to be reflected in the bibliographic data. Therefore, as part of the metadata maintenance process, metadata creators use subject authority data.

When participants of the international survey were asked how they use subject authority data in cataloging and metadata creation, about 95 percent of those who answered this question indicated that they use the data to select and verify terms for cataloging and indexing. Other uses include exploring, verifying, and understanding relationships among subject terms (see Figure 3.5).

The semantic survey participants use subject authority data mainly to access metadata information and to add subject terms and classification numbers to bibliographic data (Figure 3.6).

Both studies indicate that the majority of metadata creators use subject authority data during the process of metadata creation. However, additional uses include exploring and understanding relationships between concepts and between terms.

FIGURE 3.5   Use of subject authority data in cataloging and metadata creation.

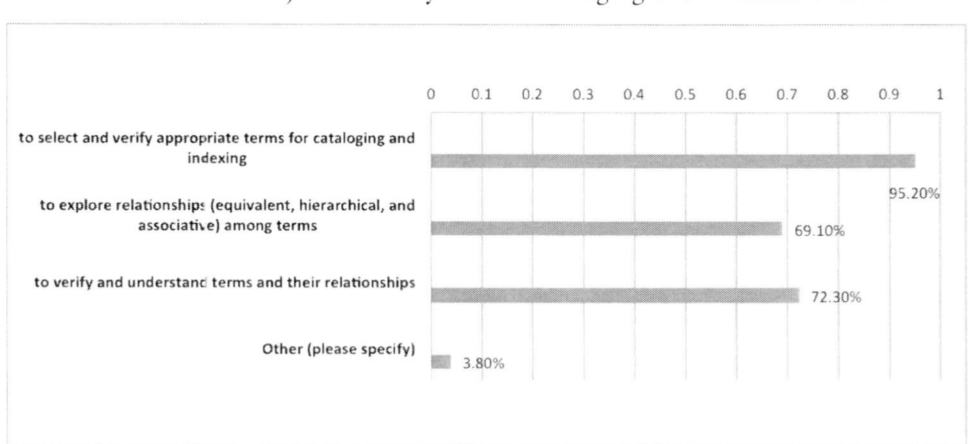

FIGURE 3.6   Use of subject authority data.

In what ways do you use the semantic tools? (ranked according the number of answers)
to access metadata information
to assign subject terms and/or class labels in metadata records

USE OF SUBJECT AUTHORITY DATA WHEN SEARCHING FOR DATA: END USERS AND PUBLIC SERVICES INFORMATION PROFESSIONALS

The majority of studies in current literature cover use of authority data as a means to find bibliographic data—the indirect use of subject data. These studies often examine user performance, behavior, understanding, and satisfaction, comparing searching using controlled vocabularies (information derived from subject authority data) versus searching using uncontrolled keyword terms.

In her study of professional searchers, Fidel (1991a, 1991b, 1991c) identified strategies for selecting terms from the indexing language using semantic relationships such as broader, narrower, and synonymous terms. From all cases of term selection, 75 percent included indexing language consultation by the searchers.

A number of studies have examined end-user queries when searching online catalogs and users' use of authority data displayed to them as sources for term selection (Sutcliffe, Ennis, & Watkinson, 2000; Hsieh-Yee, 1993). Fenichel (1981) found that all types of catalog users (professionals and end users) utilized indexing languages for term selection with experienced users selecting a significantly larger proportion of indexing language terms. A number of more recent studies have focused on the effects of thesaurus-enhanced information retrieval systems and user interaction with indexing language information, including behavior in term selection (Vakkari, 2000; Nielsen, 2002, 2004; Shiri, Revie, and Chowdhury, 2002a, 2002b; Blocks, 2004) and found that indexing languages benefit users in finding terms for query expansion and in improving search performance (Shiri, Revie, and Chowdhury, 2002b), but sometimes indexing languages are more helpful to domain experts than nonexperts (Liu, 2009). In addition, studies have examined user understanding of subject authority data as displayed to them in a catalog search interface. These studies indicate that users do not always have a clear understanding of subject authority information (Greenberg, 2004; Salaba, 2009).

In the FRSAD international survey, participants who use subject authority data in searching bibliographic information for their own needs or when helping others (end users) find bibliographic information indicated that the majority use the data available to select and to verify appropriate terms for use in search queries. Other uses include identifying relevant documents on a specified topic, modifying search queries utilizing semantic relationships,

FIGURE 3.7   Use of subject authority data in searching for bibliographic information.

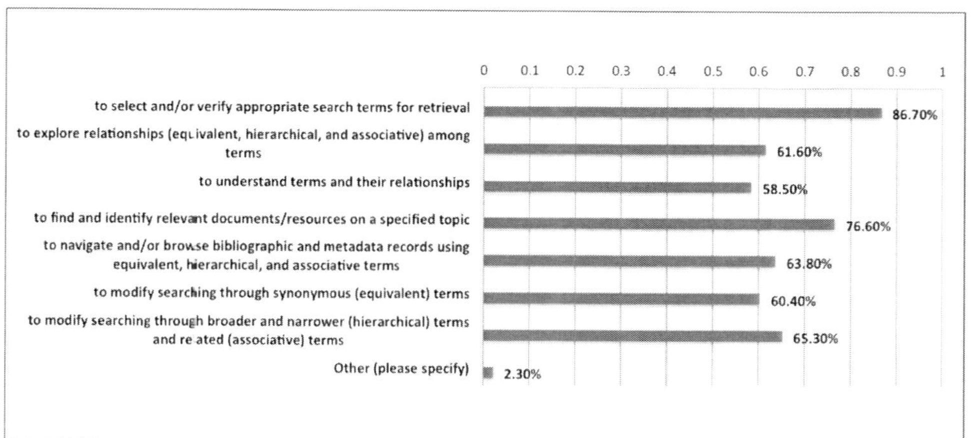

FIGURE 3.8   Use of subject authority data in searching information by semantic participants.

In what ways do you use the semantic tools? (ranked according the number of answers)
to find/ identify relevant information resources using specified terms
to access metadata information
to find /identify appropriate terms when searching for information
to navigate or modify search queries through broader and narrower terms

navigating bibliographic information using semantic relationships, and exploring and understanding subject areas and the relationships of domain subject terminology (see Figure 3.7).

The semantic survey findings include the use of subject authority data to find bibliographic data that will lead to information resources and exploration of the vocabulary through semantic relationships among concepts and terms (Figure 3.8).

USE OF SUBJECT AUTHORITY DATA BY COMPUTER APPLICATIONS

A more recent type of subject authority data user group is machines such as web services and metadata harvesting tools. Uses by machines and tools include harvesting of authority data mainly for enhancing metadata quality. One of the harvesting processes includes the transformation of metadata descriptions, a process of "modifying metadata based on the structure or values already available in statements" (Hillmann, 2008: p. 75).

Subject authority data are also used in a variety of terminology services. These services make subject authority data, such as classification data, subject headings lists, thesauri, and lists of subject terms available via web services (Vizine-Goetz, Houghton, and Childress, 2006) for different uses such as browsing, discovery, translation, mapping, subject indexing, classification, and so forth (Hillmann, 2008). Tudhhope and Binding (2006) reported on the different terminology services and how they can be used to expose vocabulary data or to allow search engines to match user search terms to vocabulary terms. They also report that even though such services exist, future work is needed for "provision of more complex services, such as semantic expansion, more advanced natural language functionality, cross-mapping provisions and data-dependent filters such as the number of postings associated with a concept."

Another indirect use of subject authority data is for co-occurrence mapping of vocabulary terms in bibliographic data. The subject data in these bibliographic records are subject authority derived data.

Overall, the most common use of subject authority data by information retrieval systems is to support searching of bibliographic data. The use of subject authority data allows query formulations and reformulations by including semantic relationships. These tools allow the user to expand the search to include all broader concepts or all narrower concepts of a given subject term.

FRSAD USER TASKS

Based on the literature, but most importantly on the two FRSAD user studies, when it comes to using subject authority data, a user may find, identify, and select a subject entity or entities, and obtain additional information on a specified subject entity. In addition, a user may choose to explore the terminology of a subject domain, the relationships that exist among these terms, and the correlation of subject terminology of one schema or vocabulary to the respective representation (term, notation, etc.) of this topic in another schema or vocabulary. For example, one may try to find the correlation of a subject term from one thesaurus to the notation within a classification schema. These findings led the FRSAD Working Group to define the following subject authority data user tasks, representing uses by all surveyed user groups. These user tasks include:

- **Find** one or more subjects and/or their appellations that correspond(s) to the user's stated criteria, using attributes and relationships;
- **Identify** a subject and/or its appellation based on its attributes or relationships (i.e., to distinguish between two or more subjects or appellations with similar characteristics and to confirm that the appropriate subject or appellation has been found);
- **Select** a subject and/or its appellation appropriate to the user's needs (i.e., to choose or reject based on the user's requirements and needs);

- **Explore** relationships between subjects and/or their appellations (e.g., to explore relationships in order to understand the structure of a subject domain and its terminology).

The *explore* user task was introduced in FRSAD as a new task, whereas the *find*, *identify*, and *select* user tasks were previously introduced in FRBR and FRAD conceptual models but were redefined in FRSAD for the subject authority data context.

The following is a list of tasks that result from placing the primary subject authority data user tasks (*find*, *identify*, *select*, and *explore*) in the context of different user groups as they relate to interacting only with subject authority data. The activities of using subject authority data to access bibliographic data are covered by FRBR. In the following examples, text within double quotation marks represents a term; a topic or subject is referred by English text within curly brackets {}. Single quotation marks are used for types of subjects.

The FIND Task

The FRSAD FIND task is defined as "using the data to find one or more subjects and/or their appellations that correspond(s) to the user's stated criteria, using attributes and relationships." One use scenario would be using subject authority data to **find** a topic or a set of topics based on the user's search criteria. For example, a user is looking for a topic of the type 'element' within the chemistry field; a user is looking for topics that are particular Indo-European languages (for example, {French language}) using the hierarchical relationships.

A second scenario under the FIND task includes using subject authority to **find** a term or a set of terms for a topic. For example, a user is looking for the Dewey Decimal Classification (DDC) number for the topic {mountain lions} (as it is referred to in English). Or, a user is looking for the preferred term in the *Sears List of Subject Headings* for the topic {maple trees} (as commonly referred to in English).

The IDENTIFY Task

The FRSAD IDENTIFY user task is defined as "using the data to identify a subject and/or its appellation based on their attributes or relationships." There are two scenarios illustrated here, one for identifying topics and one for identifying terms. First, a user wants to confirm that the topic sought is the same as the topic found or wants to distinguish between two similar topics. In this case the user uses subject authority data to **identify** a topic. For example, using subject authority data, a user wants to identify whether the topic {solar greenhouse} or the topic {sunspace} is more appropriate for her specified information need. In the second scenario, a user wants to confirm that the term found is the same as the one sought or to distinguish between two similar terms. Here the user is using subject authority data to **identify** a term. For example, using information available as subject authority data, a user wants to verify whether "middle ages" is the appropriate term in a KOS.

The SELECT Task

The FRSAD SELECT task is defined as "using the data to select a subject and/or its appellation appropriate to the user's needs." A user may use subject authority data to **select** a topic from a set of found topics or a term from a set of found terms. For example, using subject authority data, a user decides to select the topic {sweet cherry} to more appropriately represent the aboutness of a resource than its broader topic {cherry}. Here the user selects a topic at the appropriate level of specificity from a hierarchy of related topics. In the same matter, a user **selects** the preferred term among equivalent terms within a particular subject authority system to use in searching or in assigning access points. For example, a user selects the preferred "aquarelle (technique)" among "transparent watercolor," "geaquarelleerd," or "water-colour, transparent" found in the *Art & Architecture Thesaurus* to assign it a subject term for an information resource.

It is also possible that a computer application may **select** all terms from a particular subject authority data system via web terminology services that have been assigned as subjects in a set of bibliographic records.

The EXPLORE Task

The FRSAD EXPLORE task is defined as "using the data in order to explore relationships between subjects and/or their appellations." One can use subject authority data to explore relationships between topics or between terms. A user can **explore** the relationships between two or more topics within the same subject authority system, for example, the associative relationships of the topic {comedians} and other related topics. When a user is exploring the relationship of the term "bluelines (whiteprints)" to the term "blueline prints" in the *Art and Architecture Thesaurus* (AAT), subject authority data is used to explore the relationships between two terms within the same subject authority system.

A user can also use subject authority data to **explore** the correlation of topics or terms between two or more subject authority systems. For example, one can explore the correlation of the topic {deafness} between the Library of Congress Subject Headings (LCSH) and the *Sears List of Subject Headings*. Or, one can explore the correlation between the *Medical Subject Headings* (MeSH) term "skin pigmentation" and the National Library of Medicine (NLM) classification numbers.

Last, a user can use subject authority data to **explore** the structure of a subject domain within a subject authority system. For example, a user uses subject authority data to explore how the domain {information retrieval} is represented within the *American Society for Information Science and Technology (ASIS&T) Thesaurus.*

Looking at the above user tasks collectively, we can follow the different stages of subject authority data use: An information resource becomes available and acquired by an information agency. The metadata creator needs to create a description and provide different means to provide access to this resource. As a part of this description, a representation of the intellectual content is determined during the conceptual analysis. The metadata professional decides on the aboutness and needs to translate the results of this analysis into particular subject authority data. At this stage the metadata professional **finds** candidate topics, **explores** the relationships to other topics and **selects** the most appropriate topics that best represent what the resource covers, and then **finds**, **identifies**, and **selects** the preferred terms to express the selected concepts and includes them as access points in the resource description. Once this process is complete and the resource is available for discovery by end users, they may interact with the retrieval system's interface to **find** topics to **explore** and **identify** as appropriate for their information need. Next, users need to **identify** and **select** the system's preferred term or combination of terms to enter as their search terms. Users may also continue to **explore** relationships and **identify** and **select** additional topics or terms to reformulate or expand their search.

As we can observe in this scenario, it is important to note that while in some cases the users' information needs are limited to authority data only, in most cases users will utilize subject authority data to *find, identify, select,* and/or *obtain* bibliographic data or Group 1 entities as specified by the FRBR user tasks.

REFERENCES

Alpi, Kristine. (2005). "Expert Searching in Public Health." *Journal of the Medical Library Association* 93 (1): 97–103.

Blocks, D. (2004). *A Qualitative Study of Thesaurus Integration for End-user Searching.* University of Glamorgan.

Fenichel, C. H. (1981). "Online Searching: Measures That Discriminate among Users with Different Types of Experiences." *Journal of the American Society for Information Science* 32 (1): 23–32.

Fidel, R. (1991a). "Searchers' Selection of Search Keys: I. The Selection Routine." *Journal of the American Society for Information Science* 42 (7): 490–500.

Fidel, R. (1991b). "Searchers' Selection of Search Keys: II. Controlled Vocabulary or Free-text Searching." *Journal of the American Society for Information Science* 42 (7): 501–14.

Fidel, R. (1991c). "Searchers' Selection of Search Keys: III. Searching Styles.: *Journal of the American Society for Information Science* 42 (7): 515–27.

Greenberg, Jane. (2004). "User Comprehension and Searching with Information Retrieval Thesauri." *Cataloging & Classification Quarterly* 37 (3/4): 103–20.

Hillmann, Diane. (2008). "Metadata Quality: From Evaluation to Augmentation." *Cataloging and Classification Quarterly* 46 (1): 65–80.

Hsieh-Yee, I. (1993). "Effects of Search Experience and Subject Knowledge on the Search Tactics of Novice and Experienced Searchers." *Journal of the American Society for Information Science* 44 (3): 161–74.

Hunter, R. (1991). "Successes and Failures of Patrons Searching the Online Catalog at a Large Academic Library: A Transaction Log Analysis." *Reference Quarterly* 30, 395–402.

Liu, Ying-Hsang. (2009). *The Impact of MeSH (Medical Subject Headings) Terms on Information Seeking Effectiveness*. Doctoral Dissertation. Available at: http://csusap.csu.edu.au/~yingliu/YHLiu_ThesisFinalVersion.pdf

Nielsen, M. L. (2002). *The Word Association Method: A Gateway to Word-task Based Retrieval*. Abo, Finland: Abo Akademi University Press.

Nielsen, M. L. (2004). "Task Based Evaluation of Associative Thesaurus in Real-life Environment." In *Proceedings of the American Society for Information Science and Technology*, 41: 437–447.

Peters, T. A., and Kurth, M. (1991). "Controlled and Uncontrolled Vocabulary Subject Searching in an Academic Library Online Catalog." *Information Technology and Libraries* 27, 201–211.

Salaba, Athena. (2009). "End-User Understanding of Indexing Language Information." *Cataloging & Classification Quarterly* 47 (1): 23–51.

Shiri, A. A., Revie, C., and Chowdhury, G. (2002a). "Assessing the Impact of User Interaction with Thesaural Knowledge Structures: A Quantitative Analysis Framework." In *Proceedings International Society for Knowledge Organization Conference 8*, edited by M. J. Lopez-Huertas and F. J. Munoz-Fernandez, pp. 493–99. Granada, Spain.

Shiri, A. A., Revie, C., and Chowdhury, G. (2002b). "Thesaurus-assisted Search Term Selection and Query Expansion: A Review of User-centered Studies." *Knowledge Organization* 29 (1): 1–19.

Sutcliffe, A. G., Ennis, M., and Watkinson, S. J. (2000). "Empirical Studies of End-user Information Searching." *Journal of the American Society for Information Science* 51 (13): 1211–31.

Tudhhope, Douglas, and Ceri Binding. (2006). "Toward Terminology Services: Experiences with a Pilot Web Service Thesaurus Browser." *Bulletin of the American Society for Information Science and Technology*, June/July. Available at http://www.asis.org/Bulletin/Jun-06/vizine-goetz_houghton_childress.html.

Vakkari, P. (2000). "Cognition and Changes of Search Terms and Tactics during Task Performance: A Longitudinal Case Study." In *Proceedings of the RIAO'2000 Conference: Content-based Multimedia Information Access*, pp. 894–907. Paris: C.I.D.

Vizine-Goetz, Diane, Andrew Houghton, and Eric Childress. (2006). "Web Services for Controlled Vocabularies." *Bulletin of the American Society for*

Information Science and Technology, June/July. Available at http://www.asis
.org/Bulletin/Jun-06/vizine-goetz_houghton_childress.html.
Wilkes, Adeline W., and Antoinette Nelson. (1995). "Subject searching in two
online catalogs: Authority control vs non-authority control." *Cataloging &*
Classification Quarterly 20 (4): 57–79.
Yu, Holly, and Margo Young. (2004). "The Impact of Web Search Engines on
Subject Searching in OPAC." *Information Technology and Libraries* 23 (4):
168–80.

CHAPTER 4

Modeling Approaches of Aboutness

This chapter describes earlier theoretical contributions to modeling the subject relationship. It starts with the description of FRBR and FRAD, the first two models of the FRBR family, focusing only on the parts that deal with the subject relationship. Section "Examples of Other Modeling Approaches" is devoted to other examples, which illustrate different aspects of modeling— from the theoretical foundations of classification systems to general discussions.

FUNCTIONAL REQUIREMENTS FOR BIBLIOGRAPHIC RECORDS (FRBR)

FRBR defines the four basic user tasks that should be supported by bibliographic data (FRBR, 1998):

- using the data to <u>find</u> materials that correspond to the user's stated search criteria (e.g., in the context of a search for all documents on a given subject or a search for a recording issued under a particular title);

- using the data retrieved to <u>identify</u> an entity (e.g., to confirm that the document described in a record corresponds to the document sought by the user or to distinguish between two texts or recordings that have the same title);

- using the data to <u>select</u> an entity that is appropriate to the user's needs (e.g., to select a text in a language the user understands or to choose a version of a computer program that is compatible with the hardware and operating system available to the user);

- using the data in order to acquire or <u>obtain</u> access to the entity described (e.g., to place a purchase order for a publication, to submit a request for the loan of a copy of a book in a library's collection, or to access online an electronic document stored on a remote computer).

FRBR deals with subject access only in very general terms. The subject relationship ("has as subject") is shown in Figure 4.1.

The diagram is followed by the definition of Group 3 (FRBR, 1998, Section 3.1.3):

The entities in the third group (outlined in bold in Figure 3.3) represent an additional set of entities that serve as the subjects of works. The group includes concept (an abstract notion or idea), object (a material thing), event (an action or occurrence), and place (a location).

FIGURE 4.1   Group 3 entities and "subject" relationships (originally published as Figure 3.3 in FRBR, 1998).

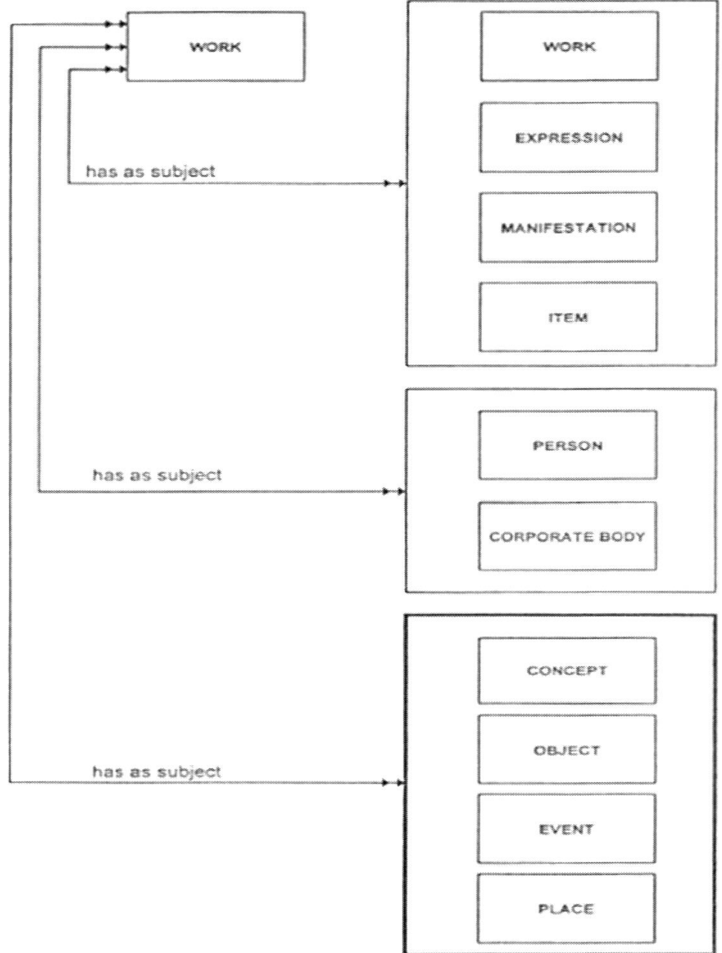

The diagram depicts the "subject" relationships between entities in the third group and the work entity in the first group. The diagram indicates that a work may have as its subject one or more than one concept, object, event, and/or place.

Conversely, a concept, object, event, and/or place may be the subject of one or more than one work.

The diagram also depicts the "subject" relationships between work and the entities in the first and second groups. The diagram indicates that a work may have as its subject one or more than one work, expression, manifestation, item, person, and/or corporate body.

The subject relationship is further defined in Section 5.3.2 (FRBR, 1998):

The entities in all three groups are connected to the work entity by a subject relationship. The "has as subject" relationship indicates that any of the entities in the model, including work itself, may be the subject of a work. Stated in slightly different terms, the relationship indicates that a work may be about a concept, an object, an event, or place; it may be about a person or corporate body; it may be about an expression, a manifestation, or an item; it may be about another work. The logical connection between a work and a related subject entity serves as the basis both for identifying the subject of an individual work and for ensuring that all works relevant to a given subject are linked to that subject.

The Group 3 entities (*object, concept, event,* and *place*) are therefore defined as an *additional* set of entities (i.e., in addition to Group 1 and Group 2 entities; emphasis added).

Discussion

It is necessary to point out that there is a common misunderstanding in the library and information science (LIS) community that, in the context of the subject relationship, Group 1 entities (*work, expression, manifestation,* and *item*) as well as Group 2 (*person, corporate body,* and FRAD *family*) are subsumed into Group 3. Such an interpretation is wrong and is not supported in the FRBR report.

Two paragraphs in the FRBR study explicitly address the need for a further study, addressing the entities that are described in authority data:

> Data associated with persons, corporate bodies, titles, and subjects are analysed only to the extent that they function as headings or index entries for the records describing bibliographic entities. The present study does not analyse those additional data associated with persons, corporate bodies, works, and subjects that are typically recorded only in authority records. (Section 2.2)
>
> The model could be extended to cover the additional data that are normally recorded in authority records. In particular, further analysis is needed of the entities that are the centre of focus for subject authorities, thesauri, and classification schemes, and of the relationships between those entities. (Section 1.3)

The IFLA FRBR study group was therefore aware of the need for a further development of the model in the area of subject access. One of the members, Tom Delsey, published an article (Delsey, 2005) in which he "explicitly highlights the aspects of FRBR that need to be re-examined as part of a more intensive analysis of subject access" (p. 49). The proposed reexamination should have the objective to ensure:

- that the scope of the entities defined in the models is sufficient to cover everything that a user of the library catalog might view as a "subject";

- that the attributes that come into play in the construction and use of subject authority records are adequately covered;

- that the models provide a clear and pragmatic representation of the relationships that are reflected through subject access points in bibliographic records as well as those reflected in the syndetic structure of thesauri, subject heading lists, and classification schemes. (Delsey, 2005)

As the first step Delsey compares the entities defined in FRBR and in the <indecs> project (Rust and Bide, 2000; described in the next section). Because the <indecs> framework is supposed to represent an exhaustive set of entities, all entities of the universe could be mapped to it. In his analysis, Delsey observes that one aspect seems to be missing from FRBR—the static relation or "situation." He looks further into FRBR *object* and agrees that a refined definition is probably necessary, bringing FRBR *object* closer to <indecs> *percept*, that is, anything perceived with the senses and therefore clearly delineated from FRBR *concept*. Delsey also discusses the possible need of defining animals (when acting as subjects) as entities in their own right versus leaving them undifferentiated within the broad category of *objects*.

While FRBR *event* is supposed to subsume time or, more specifically, time periods, Delsey also acknowledges the need to define "time" as an entity in its own right in an extended FRBR model.

In the part devoted to attributes, the need for detailed analysis is expressed. An additional attribute of *concept*, "type of concept," is proposed to enable more detailed specification, such as concept of abstraction, concept of living organism, and so forth. It is interesting to see that here Delsey somewhat conflates the two meanings of "concept": FRBR *concept* ("an abstract notion or idea") and "concept" as defined by Buizza and Guerrini ("a unit of thought, each of the single elements which make up the subject") (Buizza and Guerrini, 2002; see Section 4.3.4).

Finally, Delsey discusses the relationships. In addition to the high-level relationships that occur between all instances of any two classes of entities and are an integral part of the model, he specifically looks into the relationships that occur between particular instances only. He had already noticed that the so-called equivalence relationships occur between instances of appellations and not subjects themselves.

Another important contribution of Delsey (2005) is his point that genre, form, function, and so forth, often found in current controlled vocabularies, are not aspects of aboutness and therefore not applicable in the context of the "has as subject" relationship.

FUNCTIONAL REQUIREMENTS FOR AUTHORITY RECORDS (FRAD)

The Working Group on Functional Requirements and Numbering of Authority Records (FRANAR) was established in April 1999 by the IFLA Division of Bibliographic Control. The Working Group had three terms of reference (FRAD, 2009, p. 7):

1. To define functional requirements of authority records, continuing the work that the "Functional requirements of bibliographic records" for bibliographic systems initiated;

2. To study the feasibility of an International Standard Authority Data Number (ISADN), to define possible use and users, to determine for what types of authority records such an ISADN is necessary, to examine the possible structure of the number and the type of management that would be necessary;

3. To serve as the official IFLA liaison to and work with other interested groups concerning authority files: <indecs> (Interoperability of Data in E-Commerce Systems), ICA/CDS (International Council on Archives Committee on Descriptive Standards; later, International Council on Archives Committee on Best Practices and Professional Standards), ISO/TC46 for international numbering and descriptive standards, CERL (Consortium of European Research Libraries), etc.

The document prepared by the FRANAR Working Group addresses the first term of reference, extends the FRBR model, and identifies potential changes to the FRBR model.

While the FRANAR Working Group has included some aspects of subject authorities in the model, it has not undertaken the full analysis that the FRBR Study Group envisioned.

More specifically, the FRAD conceptual model has been designed to (FRAD, 2009, p. 13):

- provide a clearly defined, structured frame of reference for relating the data that are recorded by authority record creators to the needs of the users of that data;

- assist in an assessment of the potential for international sharing and use of authority data both within the library sector and beyond.

In FRAD, the user tasks are defined as (FRAD, 2009, Chapter 6):

- **Find:** Find an entity or set of entities corresponding to stated criteria (i.e., to find either a single entity or a set of entities using an attribute or combination of attributes or a relationship of the entity as the search criteria); or to explore the universe of bibliographic entities using those attributes and relationships.

- **Identify:** Identify an entity (i.e., to confirm that the entity represented corresponds to the entity sought, to distinguish between two or more entities with similar characteristics); or to validate the form of name to be used for a controlled access point.

- **Contextualize:** Place a person, corporate body, work, etc., in context; clarify the relationship between two or more persons, corporate bodies, works, etc.; or clarify the relationship between a person, corporate body, etc., and a name by which that person, corporate body, etc., is known (e.g., name used in religion versus secular name).

- **Justify:** Document the authority data creator's reason for choosing the name or form of name on which a controlled access point is based.

Two new user tasks are added; **contextualize** addresses the often-expressed need to cover navigation as a separate task, and **justify** serves the librarians (not end users) to record their decisions.

Discussion

In the context of the subject relationship, FRAD does not provide many details. All Group 3 entities are listed, but no additional analysis of attributes or relationships was performed because another working group (FRSAR) was established in 2005 and both were active in parallel. There is one important detail, though: the "has as subject" relationship is completely removed from the model and is replaced by a "subject" attribute of *work* (In FRAD Section 4.4, "Attributes of a Work," it is listed: "Subject of the Work" with definition: "The subject aspects of the work and its content. Includes information about the subject of the work. Includes classification numbers" [FRAD, 2009, p. 44]). This is a possible modeling decision, as relationships can be modeled as attributes and in some modeling methodologies (for example, object-oriented), attributes and relationships are treated the same. However, making *subject* an attribute of *work* and not an entity on its own makes it impossible to consistently model appellations (names, labels) and their attributes separate from entities of which they are appellations. It remains a question as to why the FRBR Group 3 entities (*object*, *concept*, *event*, *place*) are mentioned in FRAD at all because they are, in the FRBR model, only defined in the context of the "has as subject" relationship. With no "has as subject" in FRAD these entities are unnecessary.

EXAMPLES OF OTHER MODELING APPROACHES

<indecs>

<indecs> ("interoperability of data in e-commerce systems") was a project partly funded by the European Community Info 2000 initiative and by several organizations representing music, intellectual rights management, text publishing, authors, libraries, and other sectors in 1998 through 2000. The summary of the theoretical background is given in a much-cited report (Rust and Bide, 2000).

FIGURE 4.2   General view of the <indecs> model (Based on Rust and Bide, 2000).

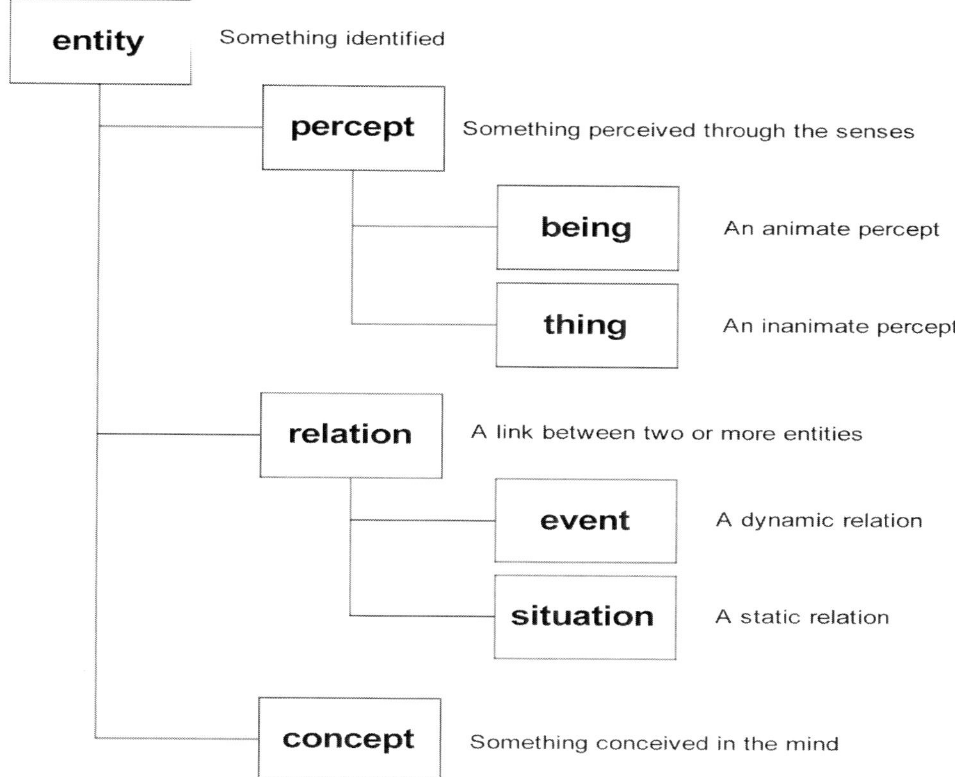

The project provided an analysis of the requirements for metadata for e-commerce content (intellectual property) in the network environment. The result is a reference model that defines the basic entities (*parties, creations, transactions*) but at the same time provides a general framework that supports three distinct but overlapping views of entities: the general view and two specific views (commerce view and intellectual property view).

In the model (Figure 4.2) three basic entity types are defined: those that are perceived with the senses (*percepts*), those that are conceived in the mind (*concepts*), and those in which two or more of these are connected (*relations*). The percepts are further divided into animate (*beings*) and inanimate (*things*), and relations are dynamic (*events*) and static (*situations*).

Discussion

<indecs>, while different in scope and focused on e-commerce, provides a new approach to general modeling of the universe. We are interested only in the general view and not the detailed modeling of attributes and relationships that are needed to identify and record transactions of e-commerce.

In this model the *event* plays a special role as the mechanism of creating and connecting instances of entities. In this aspect the <indecs> model is similar to the CIDOC (International Council of Museums) Conceptual Reference Model (CRM) developed for the museum community, which is also event based.

Ranganathan's Facets

Ranganathan's aim in developing his famous colon classification (CC) was to provide a general theory for classification. Because most subjects can be seen as compounds, Ranganathan proposes five fundamental aspects or facets: personality, matter, energy, space, and time (PMEST). Space and time are self-explanatory. Energy covers activities, processes, operations that consume mental or physical effort, and materials. Matter covers what occupies space or what is experienced by the five senses. Personality is not explicitly defined but is used when other facets are not appropriate. It is the core or root element found in most specific subjects.

Discussion

Colon classification represents a highly theoretical approach regarded highly by many, but not widely implemented. Its significance is in its influence on the theory of classification and its approach to concept analysis.

Information Coding Classification by Dahlberg

Ingetraut Dahlberg describes her Information Coding Classification (ICC) as consisting of nine general object areas according to the principle of evolution (Dahlberg, 1998):

1. Form and structure area
2. Matter and energy area
3. Cosmos and earth area
4. Bio area
5. Human area
6. Socio area
7. Economics and production area
8. Science and information area
9. Culture area

These nine areas have an evolutionary sequence and an internal structure of 3×3: areas 1 to 3 deal with nonliving matter, 4 to 6 are about living organisms, and 7 to 9 are products of human beings and society: material, intellectual, and metaphysical "artifacts."

When further specifying the contents of the nine areas, a series of aspects or facets are proposed:

1. General and theoretical concepts
2. Object-related concepts (also elements, parts, characteristics of objects, kinds of objects)
3. Activity-related concepts (states, processes, operations)

4–6. Concepts related to specialties of the objects and/or activities in facets 2 and 3

7. Concepts of influences on 2 and 3 from outside ("instrumental," technical relationship)
8. Concepts of the use of 2 and 3 in other fields ("potential," resource orientation, application relationship)
9. Concepts concerning the knowledge about 1 through 8 when it is distributed by persons, societies, documents, or used in educational purposes and in other kinds of applications ("actualization," synthesizing, environmental relationship) (Dahlberg, 1998).

These facets can be applied on all levels of abstraction in a subject group or subject field.

ICC was designed as a theoretical superstructure of a universal system, and the author proposed its use as a switching mechanism between the five widely used classification systems: Dewey Decimal Classification (DDC), Universal Decimal Classification (UDC); Library of Congress Classification (LCC), Bliss Bibliographic Classification (BC), and CC.

Discussion

ICC is a highly theoretical work, interesting in its high-level systematization of knowledge units. It is very important for development of universal controlled vocabularies, particularly classification systems. On the other hand it may not be directly useful for modeling the indexing or cataloging process and particularly not for the analysis of end-user subject searching.

Buizza and Guerrini

Reporting on their feasibility study for the renewal of the *Soggetario* (Italian subject headings), Buizza and Guerrini (2002) build on FRBR and amplify the user tasks (in context of subject searching) as:

- *Find* the works on a given subject
- *Find* the works in which a concept is significantly treated
- *Select* a work by its main subject only
- *Lead* to a search for works on related subjects
- *Lead* to a search for works in which related or connected subjects are handled

While recognizing the links of semantic indexing to the linguistic and cultural context of the local environment, they particularly emphasize the need for international debate and the development of an international document.

The authors start their modeling approach with a theoretical introduction (p. 35):

The subject belongs to the real world as a conceptual representation of the indexer, which represents the contents of the work in a summarized and formalized way. The subject is not an entity present in the work and extracted from it, nor is it a preconstructed entity which exists in its own right. It exists as a conceptual nucleus of information created in order to mediate between the theme developed in the work and the universe of cultural and informational discourses which originate the requests for the bibliographic enquiries. It is a logical entity which persists through the various relationships with diverse works, independent of the expressions and manifestations in which they occur, and allows us to recognize and relate the works which present the same basic theme and to distinguish them from those which develop different themes.

Two entities are defined:

- The *subject*: the topic, the basic theme of the work, the summarization of the main concepts
- The *concept*: a unit of thought, each of the single elements which make up the subject

The *subject* is therefore defined as the overall topic of a work, and *concept* is an atomic component of that topic. It has to be emphasized here that *concept* in this context is in no way related to *concept* in FRBR (where it denotes "an abstract notion or idea").

The authors then continue developing the model by listing possible categories or types of *concept*:

- Concept of object (material thing)
- Concept of abstraction
- Concept of living organism
- Concept of person
- Concept of corporate body
- Concept of work
- Concept of matter/material
- Concept of property/quality
- Concept of action

- Concept of process
- Concept of event
- Concept of place
- Concept of time

The appellations (labels) are the only attributes of the two entity types defined: *verbal designation* for *subject* (which is the subject heading string) and *term* and *qualification* for *concept*.

Three groups of relationships are proposed:

- *Primary relationships*: between the subject and the concepts that compose it
- *Intrasubject relationships* between concepts that compose the same subject
- *Extrasubject relationships* between concepts independently of the subject in which they are used. They are further developed as:
  - *Generic hierarchical relationships*
  - *Partitive hierarchical relationships*
  - *Antonymous relationships*
  - *Associative relationships.*

Discussion

This is an example of a cataloger- or indexer-centered approach: the analysis is focused on the process of determining appropriate index terms, specifically subject heading strings. Creation and maintenance of controlled vocabularies and user perspective (i.e., searching for works about a topic) are not specifically addressed. The study preceded FRSAD and was an important resource in the analysis.

Because the focus of the FRSAD work was broader than the subject headings lists, the FRSAR working group was particularly interested in the categories of concepts. The categories in the list are obviously overlapping (e.g., *living organism* and *person*; *work* and *abstraction*), but on the other hand they also point out how insufficient the FRBR Group 3 entities are. Buizza and Guerrini also propose a network of relationships between concepts and not the traditional division of headings and subdivisions of, for example, LCSH. In this approach they are close to Faceted Application of Subject Terminology (FAST), described in the next section.

FAST

FAST was a joint development of the Library of Congress and Online Computer Library Center (OCLC). The goal of the project was to extend the use of LCSH to the metadata created for online digital information.

FAST is a controlled vocabulary based on LCSH and is focused on applications beyond traditional library catalogs, particularly for Dublin Core records. In line with Dublin Core premises, such a system should be (Chan and O'Neill, 2010):

- simple;
- easy for indexers and catalogers to assign and maintain;
- easy for searchers to understand and search; and
- flexible enough for use across disciplines and in various knowledge discovery and access environments, not the least of which is the online public access catalog (OPAC)

The drawback of using LCSH in such environments and for such purposes is LCSH's complex set of application rules, which only professionally trained catalogers can understand and apply appropriately. While retaining the vocabulary of LCSH, OCLC decided to develop a simpler, faceted syntax governing the application of subject headings. Such a faceted system can simplify the assignment process and is more intuitive for the users. In addition, computer technology can be used in vocabulary maintenance and subject authority control. Chan and O'Neill (2010, p. 22) list the most important criteria when choosing a controlled vocabulary (in addition to the two obvious ones: subject domain and language): compatibility with existing metadata, ease of assignment, retrieval effectiveness, and cost of maintenance.

FAST proposes seven subject facets and one form/genre facet:

- Topic
- Place
- Time
- Event
- Person
- Corporate body
- Title of work
- Form/genre

The headings belonging to the *topic* facet are further subdivided into the following types:

- Concepts and objects
- Form/genre as subject
- Fictitious, legendary, and mythological characters
- Named animals
- Imaginary places and organizations

- Geologic periods
- Other entities bearing proper names

With the exception of chronological headings, all possible headings are pre-established and represented by authority headings. FAST headings for complex subjects are created by precoordination as phrases containing multiple concepts or main heading/subdivision combinations, but only within the same facet. Headings from different facets are combined during searching (so-called postcoordination). Complex headings are created as (examples of headings in parentheses) (Chan and O'Neill, 2010):

- Adjectival phrase ("Plant inspection," "Wildlife recovery")
- Enumeration or lists ("Decoration and ornament," "Camp sites, facilities, etc.")
- Relationships expressed as conjunction ("Books and reading," "Mass media and gays")
- Phrases containing prepositions ("Internet in library reference services," "Oil pollution of groundwater")
- Headings with subdivisions ("Life skills—Testing," "Sound recordings—Remixing")
- Combinations of techniques ("Illumination of books and manuscripts," "Newly independent states—Diplomatic and consular service")
- Other complex headings ("Children—Books and reading—Government policy," "Jewish religious education of children with disabilities")

Three types of relationships are introduced in FAST: equivalence, hierarchical, and associative. Equivalence is established between synonyms, variant spellings, full forms and abbreviations, terms in different languages, and narrower and broader terms when the narrower term is not used as a heading. Hierarchical relationships include generic, partial, and instance, but also compound and complex relationships between complex concepts and their components (establishing "Crime" as a broader concept of "Education and crime"). Associative relationships are established particularly to link two concepts with overlapping meanings, to link a discipline and the object studied, and to link a class of persons and their field of endeavor.

Discussion

In the context of FRSAD, the FAST facets are particularly interesting. While the form/genre facet is not within the context of aboutness, other facets can be directly related to the analysis performed by the FRSAR Working Group. In terms of FRBR, Group 2 entities (*person, corporate body*) are included; of Group 1 entities, only *work* is listed (assuming that "title of work" really means *work* and not its appellation). Compared to FRBR Group 3 entities, *event* and *place* are listed; *time* is added and is not subsumed into *event*. FRBR *concept* and *object* are combined into the generic facet *topic*.

It is interesting to see that the form/genre facet is clearly separated from the seven subject facets, yet among the examples of application of FAST headings (p. 212), the headings "Rock music" and "Alternative rock music" are assigned to an audio CD as topical headings instead of form/genre headings.

FAST presents a new approach in subject headings and is an important step towards a broader use of controlled vocabularies outside the traditional library domain.

REFERENCES

Buizza, P., and Guerrini, M. (2002). "A Conceptual Model for the New Soggettario: Subject Indexing in the Light of FRBR." *Cataloging & Classification Quarterly* 34 (4): 31–45.

Chan, L. M., and O'Neill, E. T. (2010). *FAST: Faceted Application of Subject Terminology*. Santa Barbara, California: Libraries Unlimited.

Dahlberg, I. (1998). "Classification Structure Principles: Investigations, Experiences, Conclusions." In *5th International ISKO Conference*, str. 80–88. Lille: Ergon.

Delsey, T. (2005). "Modeling Subject Access: Extending the FRBR and FRANAR Conceptual Models." In *FRBR: Hype or Cure-all*, edited by P. Le Boeuf str. 49–61. New York: Haworth Information.

Functional Requirement for Bibliographic Records. (1998). München: Saur.

Functional Requirements for Authority Data (FRAD). (2009). München: Saur.

Rust, G., and Bide, M. (2000). *The <indecs> Metadata Framewok: Principles, Model and Data Dictionary. Version 2*. Available at http://www.doi.org/topics/indecs/indecs_framework_2000.pdf.

CHAPTER 5

The FRSAD Model

This chapter presents the FRSAD model. Starting from the user tasks, the chapter gives an outline of the model and detailed explanation in terms of entities, attributes, and relationships.

USER TASKS

Based on the analysis described in Chapter 3, the user tasks related to subject access are defined as:

- **Find** (locate one or more subjects and/or their appellations, based on user's search criteria)
- **Identify** (distinguish between similar subjects and/or their appellations; verify that what was found corresponds to what was sought)
- **Select** (among the subjects/appellations found, choose the ones that correspond to the user's needs or context)
- **Explore** (get familiar with the domain/system and its terminology)

In most cases the user will not limit the interaction with the system to the KOS but rather will use the subjects (or rather their appellations) found, identified, and selected to gain access to the resources (i.e., works, expressions, manifestations, items) that will solve the information problem.

The FRSAD model, presented in this chapter, was designed to support these user tasks.

OUTLINE

Figure 5.1 shows the core of the FRSAD model. Entities are represented by rectangles, and relationships are indicated as lines. The arrows represent the cardinality of the basic relationships: the double arrows mean that all basic relationships are many-to-many. The relationship labels are written in both directions: the label above the line indicates the relationship from left to right, and the label below the line belongs to the reverse relationship.

FIGURE 5.1   The basic FRSAD model.

The model can be presented showing each of the basic relationships separately, as in Figures 5.2 and Figure 5.3. In this way the relationships can be analyzed separately.

Figure 5.4 positions the FRSAD model in the context of FRBR. The relationship *work* "has as subject" remains the same. The two main differences are

1. instead of three boxes (three groups of entities) indicating the range of the "has as subject" relationship, FRSAD proposes a superclass, *thema*; and

2. the split between the thing itself (*thema*) and its appellation (*nomen*) is explicitly introduced.

Thema is defined as "any entity used as a subject of a *work.*" *Nomen* is "any sign or sequence of signs (alphanumeric characters, symbols, sound, etc.) by which a *thema* is known, referred to or addressed as."

ENTITIES

Thema

Thema is defined as "any entity used as a subject of a *work*," or anything that serves as subject of a *work*. It is important to note that this entity class is not restricted to actual subjects of works within a collection but rather applies to anything that is or has the potential of being or becoming a subject. This generality enables the development of different KOS and tools and allows different implementations according to particular circumstances and needs. It also allows the KOS to include *themas* that no work in the collection has as subject.

In the context of a particular implementation, there are two aspects of *thema*. The first is the cataloger's view when cataloging a work. The second is the user's view of a bibliographic information system. The cataloger analyzes

FIGURE 5.2   Part 1: The "has as subject" relationship.

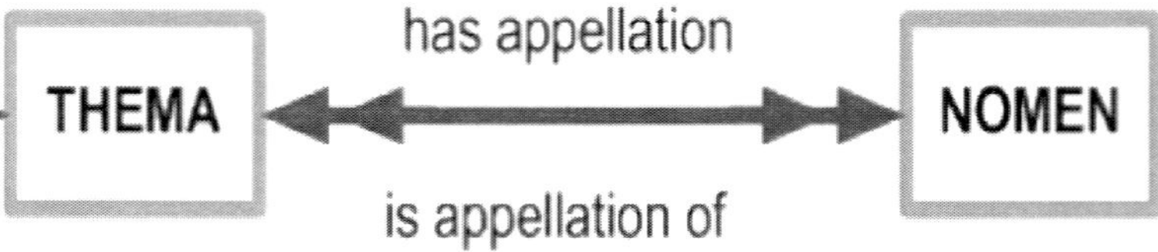

FIGURE 5.3 Part 2: The "has appellation" relationship.

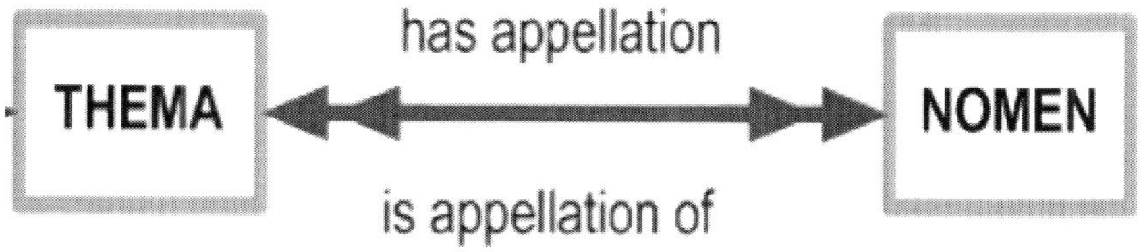

FIGURE 5.4 FRSAD in context of FRBR.

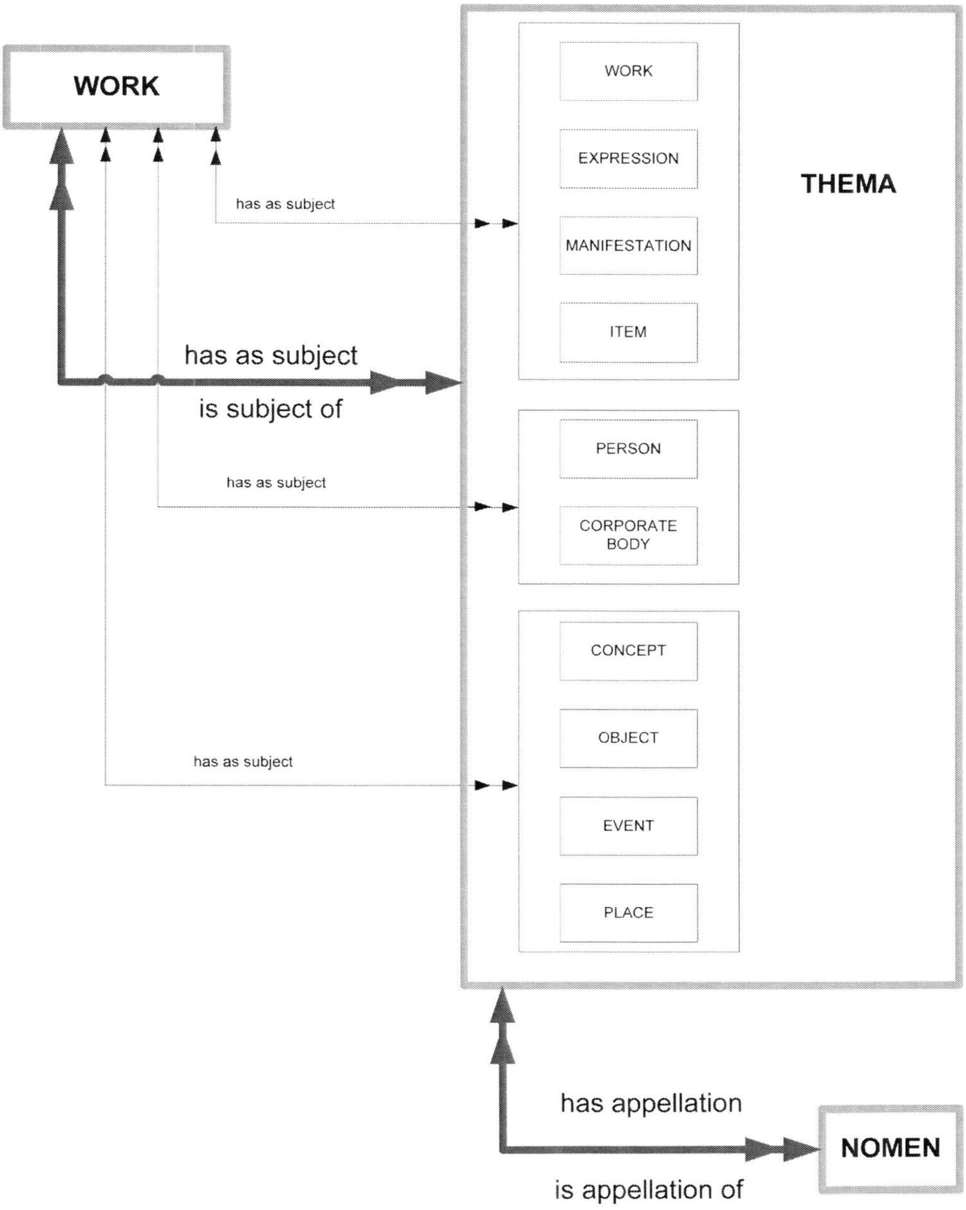

Example 5.1:

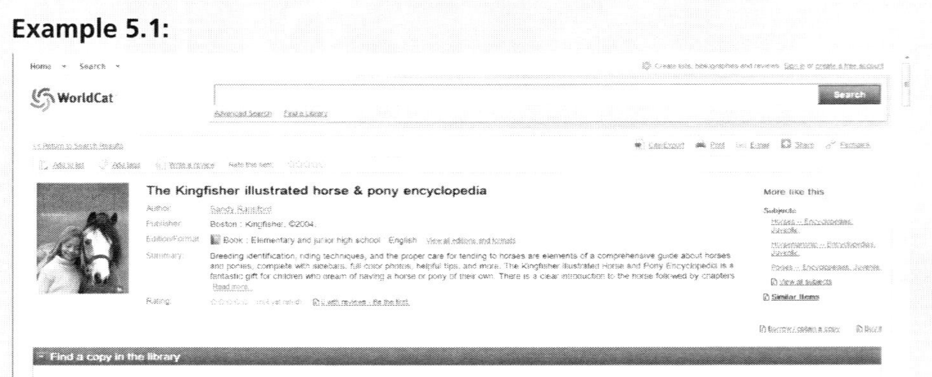

Example 5.1 is a record for a book, which is clearly about horses. Horses are therefore the *thema* of this work. At the same time, this book is also about riding, horse breeds, and horse and pony care, making these *themas* as well.

Example 5.2:

This work by Piaget (Example 5.2) is about developmental psychology or child development. It is also about cognition, imitative behavior, and play.

the content of a resource and expresses this view by assigning a *nomen* representing a *thema* from the knowledge information system. The user in a similar way analyzes his or her thematic information need. Finally, both the cataloger and the user are limited by the constraints of the KOS or the term(s) used.

Thema is therefore the totality of what a particular work is about or any of the more atomic aspects of that totality. Examples of records from WorldCat[1] (used with permission) are given here with further explanations provided under each example.

While one intuitively understands the notion of complexity of *themas* (e.g., "winter fishing in Cuyahoga River" is more complex than "cats"), there is no

---

[1]WorldCat® is a registered trademark of OCLC Online Computer Library Center, Inc.

Example 5.3:

The overall topic of this work (Example 5.3) is London, the capital of the United Kingdom. It is also about hotels and restaurants of London, museums of London, the Tower of London, Trafalgar Square, the Thames, the climate of London, and so forth.

Example 5.4:

Thema, represented in English as "Teacher certification in Alabama," as represented in three controlled vocabularies.

LCSH:

Teachers—Certification—Alabama.

FAST:

Teachers–Certification

Alabama

ERIC Thesaurus:

"Teacher Certification"

general definition of complexity. No general atomic *thema* can be agreed upon because we can always split or subdivide any *thema*. On the other hand, in each specific KOS the atomic level is specified as well as the rules of establishing complex *themas*. In a subject heading system, for example, complexity is obtained by creating subject heading strings with the rules that govern the order of subdivisions and constraints of their formation (see Example 5.4).

The intuitive notion of complexity of a *thema* is, to certain degree, also associated with the complexity of the *nomen* used for its representation. *Themas*

Example 5.5:

While linguists have proven that the (large) numbers of words for "snow" in Inuit are just an urban legend, there are examples of such words for which the English equivalent is a phrase, such as *muruaneq* for "soft deep snow" or *qanisqine* for "snow floating on water." We can claim that the phrases used in English imply a more complex concept compared to single words in Inuit.

represented by single words are perceived as simpler than *themas* represented by multiple-term words or phrases. This on its own shows that the notion of complexity depends on the language, culture, or KOS. There are considerable differences in the complexity of *nomens* for the same *thema* in different languages. What is referred to by a single word in one language may need to be described by a phrase in another. It is natural that the speakers of the former will consider the same *thema* as simple while speakers of the latter language will perceive it as complex (Example 5.5).

The *thema*-to-*thema* relationships cover the modeling of complexity in each particular system.

Nomen

In FRSAD, *nomen* is defined as "any sign or sequence of signs (alphanumeric characters, symbols, sound, etc.) by which a *thema* is known, referred to or addressed as." The definition of *nomen* is very broad, covering any form of appellation from the most common alphanumeric to sound and any visual representation. *Nomen* is therefore what we use to communicate meaning.

"Infinity," "neskončnost," and "∞" are all *nomens* for the notion of unlimitedness in mathematics. "Euro," "evro," "EUR," and "€" are all *nomens* for the European currency. In all cases they also include the sound (spoken) versions.

The notion of the split between the thing itself and the label we use to refer to it has already been described in literature. As early as 1923, Ogden and Richards (1923) published a famous triangle of meaning that illustrated the relationships among language, thought content, and referent. The graph (Figure 5.5) implies that the referent of an expression (a word or another sign or symbol) is relative to different language users.

Ogden's model was also adopted by researchers in library and information science as the basis for building subject authority systems (Dahlberg, 1992; Campbell et al, 1998).

The FRBR model does not explicitly include the appellation aspect. Appellations are modeled there as attributes of entities, for example "title of work," "title of manifestation," "name of person," and so forth. While this approach is not uncommon, it does not allow for modeling the relationships between different

FIGURE 5.5   Ogden's semiotic triangle (Ogden and Richards, 1923, p. 11, reprinted with permission) and a simple interpretation.

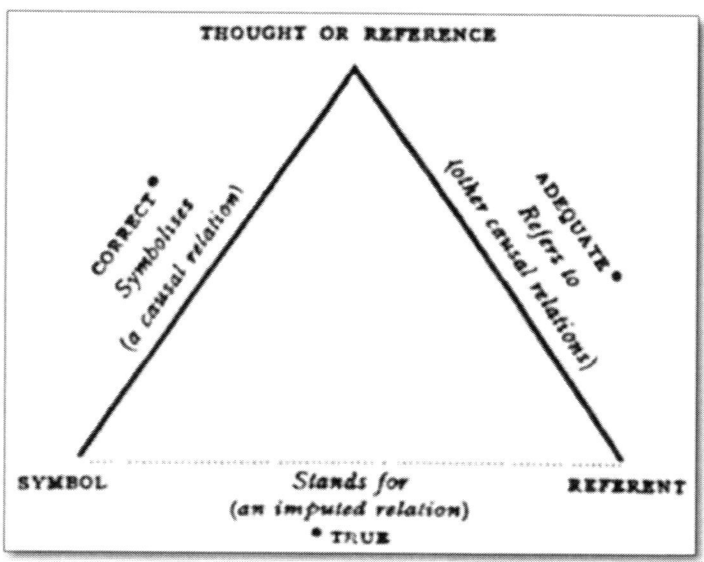

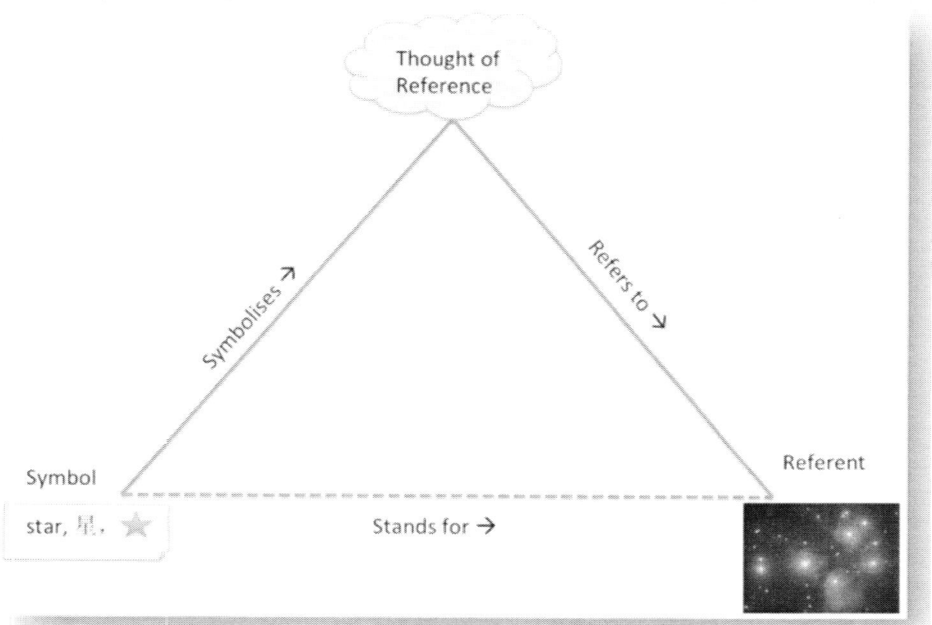

appellations, such as between the former and later name or between titles in different languages. It also prevents defining any attributes that apply to the appellation (and not the thing itself), such as language, script, or encoding of an appellation.

FRAD, on the other hand, models the appellations in a similar but not identical way compared to FRSAD. There are three appellation entities in FRAD:

name (a character or group of words and/or characters by which an entity is known in the real world); *controlled access point* (a name, term, code, etc., under which a bibliographic or authority record or reference will be found); and *identifier* (a number, code, word, phrase, logo, device, etc., that is associated with an entity and serves to differentiate that entity from other entities within the domain in which the identifier is assigned) (FRAD, 2009). FRSAD *nomen* is therefore the superclass of the three FRAD appellation entity types and in addition includes all nonalphanumeric appellations.

RELATIONSHIPS

Basic Relationships between Entities

"Has as Subject" Relationship

Figures 5.2 and 5.3 present the two basic relationships. The first, *work* "has as subject," is already defined in FRBR. It is a many-to-many relationship between instances of *works* and instances of *themas*. This means that any *work* may have several *themas* and any *thema* may be a subject of several *works*.

Let us take the previously mentioned travel book (in Section "*Thema*") as an example: the book *London* has many *themas*: hotels and restaurants of London, museums of London, the Tower of London, Trafalgar Square, the Thames, and the climate of London. This work therefore has many *themas*. At the same time, there are many other books about any of the topics listed. For example, all the following works, represented by records from WorldCat[2] (used with permission), have London as a subject:

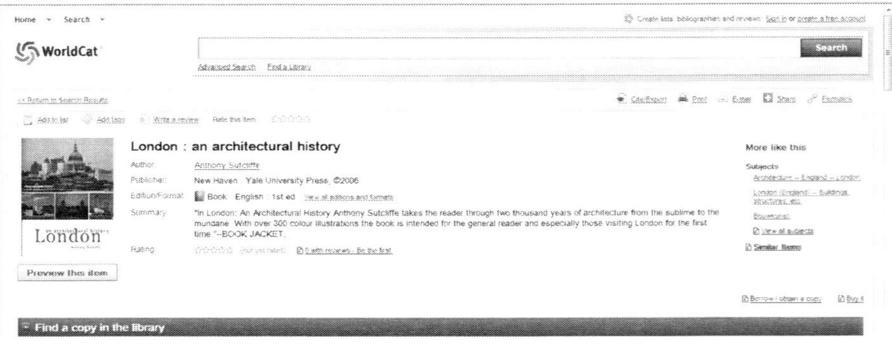

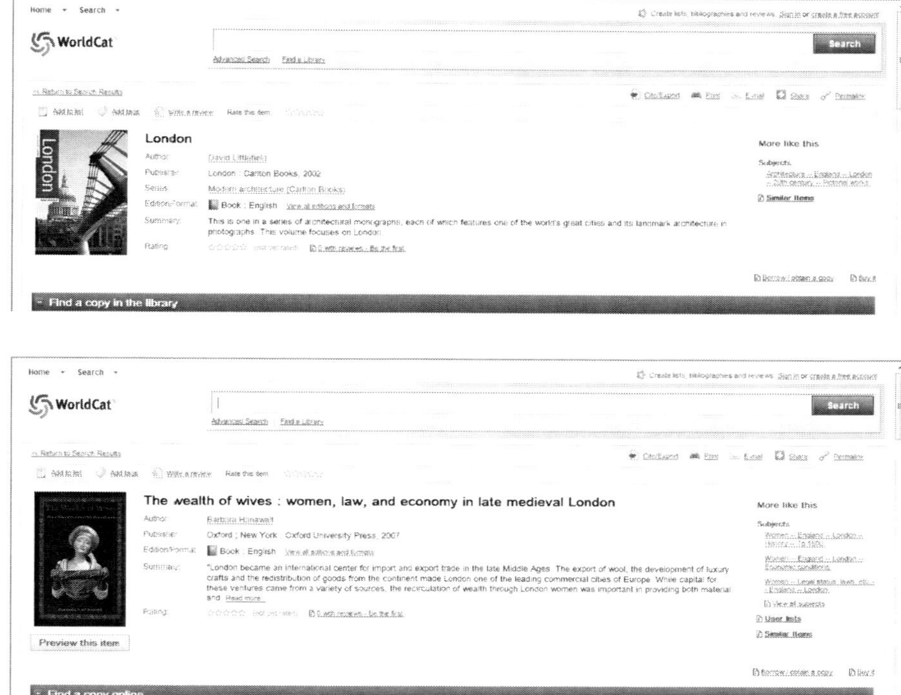

The nature of *thema* (anything serving as subject of a work) implies that there may exist *themas* that are not a subject of any *work* in a collection. On the other hand there also exist instances of *works* with no *thema*. Common examples include some musical works or abstract art. These *works* are commonly not perceived as being "about something" and for that reason the "has as subject" relation would not apply to them.

"Has Appellation" Relationship

The "has appellation/is appellation of" relationship is a new relationship introduced by FRSAD. Again, it is in general a many-to-many relationship. Any *thema* will have multiple *nomens* (e.g., in different languages, in different KOS). In a natural language, a *nomen* may be an appellation of more than one *thema*: *crane* in English is used both for an animal and a piece of construction equipment. In a controlled vocabulary, though, such a situation is avoided and each *nomen* may only be the appellation of one *thema*. To achieve this, qualifiers or other methods of disambiguation are used. Figure 5.6 shows the difference between the "has appellation/is appellation of" relationship in the natural-language environment from that in a controlled vocabulary.

There may be *nomens* that are not appellations of any *thema*, such as nonsensical words or images. There also exist *themas* with no *nomen*. Examples include things in nature that have not been discovered and, consequently, named: elementary particles or animal species obviously existed before they were

FIGURE 5.6   Illustration of the difference between the "has appellation/is appellation of" relationship in the natural-language environment and in a controlled vocabulary.

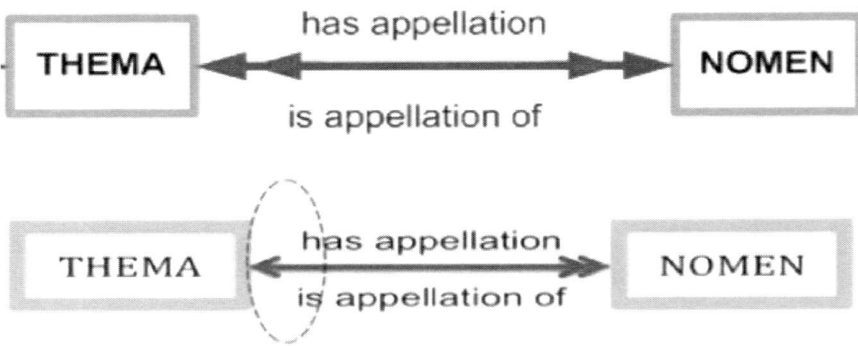

discovered and named by scientists. Cases of *themas* with no *nomen* and *nomens* representing no *thema* are beyond the scope of the FRSAD model.

Thema-to-*Thema* Relationships

The *thema*-to-*thema* relationship types are discussed here in the context of subject access points in bibliographic records as well as the construction and use of subject authority data "in the syndetic structure of thesauri, subject headings lists, and classification schemes and in the syntactic structure of indexing strings" (Delsey, 2005). The FRBR and FRAD models cover additional entity-to-entity relationships such as relationships between *works*. It should be emphasized that although this section highlights general hierarchical and associative relationships, there are other semantic relationships between and among *themas*.

Hierarchical Relationships

Hierarchical structures have been one of the fundamental components of classification schemes, subject heading systems, and thesauri for a long time and have sound roots in philosophy, logic, and scientific taxonomy. They are also widely used today in general categorization, browsing services, ontologies, and content management systems. Looking from the user tasks defined by FRSAD in relation to the bibliographic universe, hierarchical relationships are the most effective in furthering linking and navigation among *themas* and satisfying the *select* and, especially, the *explore* user tasks. To the catalogers, indexers, and searchers, the hierarchical relationships allow them to choose the appropriate level of specificity of a concept by moving to upper or lower levels (Clarke, 2001). To the end users, the hierarchical structures facilitate navigation and help them to improve their searching, especially when they have undefined or very broad information needs. The hierarchical structures also provide disambiguation functions through the hierarchical context or membership relation to satisfy the *find* and *identify* user tasks.

In KOS, the hierarchical structures reveal degrees or levels of superordination and subordination through *nomens* (usually seen as notations or terms) that represent *themas* in hierarchies, where the superordinate *thema* corresponds to a class or a whole and subordinate *themas* refer to its members or parts (NISO, 2005; Iyer, 1995). Using a classification system as an example, classes A, B, C at the same level of division are described as coordinate. Equal-level classes (A, B, C) may be grouped together into a higher-level class X. Therefore class X is superordinate to the original classes A, B, C. From another perspective, a class (X) may be divided into a number of subclasses (A, B, C), where each subclass is a subset (i.e., subordinate) of the original class. This process may be repeated and the subclasses divided into a lower level of subclasses.

Typically, the hierarchical relationship may be considered as one of three types: the generic relationship, the hierarchical whole-part relationship, and the instance relationship (ISO, 2011, Clause 10). Some concepts can belong to more than one superordinate concept simultaneously and are considered to have *polyhierarchical relationships*. Additionally, other perspective hierarchical relationships also exist (as explained in Section "Polyhierarchical, Faceted, and Perspective Hierarchical Structures").

The Generic Relationship

The *generic relationship* type used in a subject authority system can be traced from logic. The generic relationship is the logical relationship of inclusion. For example, the relationship of "passenger ship" with "ship" is expressed by the intension and extension of a concept in logic. The intension of "ship" is "vehicle for conveyance on water," indicating the internal content of a term or concept that constitutes its formal definition; its extension indicates its range of applicability by naming the particular objects that it denotes, such things as cargo ships, passenger ships, battleships, and sailing ships (*Encyclopaedia Britannica*, 2006). The relationship is also simply referred as a "kind-of;" that is, a passenger ship is a kind-of a ship. A lake, a river, or a sea can be considered as a kind-of body of water. In the computer science literature and formal ontology construction, the characteristic of "inheritance" of genus-species relationships is also widely presumed. This assumes that what is true of a given class (e.g., ship) is true of all member-classes it subsumes (cargo ships, passenger ships, battleships, and sailing ships, and so on). Using "all-some" reasoning, the genus-species relationship can be identified. A good example is that all parrots are birds; some birds are pets; but not all parrots are pets. Therefore the genus-species relationship between parrots and pets does not exist in logic (Svenonius, 2000; ISO, 2011, Clause 10.2.2.1).

The Hierarchical Whole-Part Relationship

Hierarchical relationships also exist widely in physical objects, geographical regions, hierarchical organizational structures, disciplines or fields of discourse, and other situations.

For example, anchor, deck, superstructure, and smokestack are parts of a ship. Ljubljana is part of Slovenia; Slovenia is a member of the European Union. The bed of a river and the banks are parts of a river. Compared with the "kind-of" relationship, the examples listed above can only be expressed as "part-of"; for instance, a bed of a river cannot be said to be a kind-of river but can be said to be a part-of a river. Thus the type *hierarchical whole-part relationship* needs to be introduced here to cover situations where one concept is included in another so that concepts can be organized into hierarchies.

The Instance Relationship

The *instance relationship* identifies the link between a general class of things or events (often expressed by a common name) and an individual instance of that category (often a proper noun). For example, the Yangtze River, the Black Sea, and Lake Ontario may be assigned to subordinate positions in a hierarchy of bodies of water, yet they are neither kinds-of nor parts-of bodies of waters. What they represent are specific examples or instances.

Polyhierarchical, Faceted, and Perspective Hierarchical Structures

Some *themas* can belong to more than one superordinate *thema* at the same time. These relationships can be (a) generic, as smartphones are a kind of mobile phone but are already considered in other areas and are listed as portable media players, cameras, and GPS navigation devices; (b) whole-part, as chemical physics is the branch of physics that studies chemical processes from the point of view of physics and is regarded as a subdiscipline of chemistry as well as physics; (c) more than one type, as Mercury is a planet (instance-of), the smallest planet in the solar system (part-of), and is an inferior planet (kind-of). In an astronomy classification system, Mercury may be presented in all these three hierarchies.

1. A *polyhierarchical* relationship situation usually refers to a *thema* that belongs to more than one class when one of the characteristics is introduced in classifying the concepts, such as the situation in example (a) above. For example, when classifying instruments in a music classification according to the type of instrument (instead of historical period, country, or region), "organ" can be listed under both "wind instrument" and "keyboard instrument" hierarchically. Example (b) presents a similar situation where one *thema* (chemical physics) belongs to more than one group (chemistry, physics).

2. The last example, (c), is different from the polyhierarchical situation discussed above. It introduces *faceted* analysis. In KOS and navigational interfaces, faceted analysis brings different perspectives to the same concept. For example, while ships are often categorized as sailing ship, steamship, or motorship, they are also categorized based on shape and size, building materials used, geographic origin

of the vessel, manufacturer, and other properties. A faceted structure can be formally integrated into hierarchical structures to present faceted groups or classes under the same concept.

3. Less systematic than faceted analysis, *perspective hierarchies* (Svenonius, 2000) are often seen in KOS. For example, "wind" as the bulk movement of air on Earth is studied from many points of view such as meteorology, earth science, transportation, history, power source, recreation, erosion, effects to plants and animals, damage, and so on. In KOS, depending upon the needs, "wind" may be presented in multiple positions in one system. The value of perspective hierarchies is that they provide points of view about a concept and the aspect under which it is considered (Svenonius, 2000). Other reasons to employ perspective hierarchies are that concepts and terms may be polysemantic, vague, or ambiguous (e.g., "beauty"). Hence there might be no agreement as to what genus (class) such concepts belong. Unlike the genus-species and whole-part hierarchical relationships, in which axioms are assumed and inheritable properties are possessed, perspective hierarchies bring features selected by the designer of subject vocabularies, which are selective in nature and may be implicit. Also, perspective relationships are not always exclusive and exhaustive in subject vocabularies (Svenonius, 2000). It is important in such situations to consider the requirements of literary warrant (the natural language used to describe content objects), user warrant (the language of users), and sometimes, organizational warrant (the needs and priorities of the organization) (NISO, 2005).

Associative Relationships

When *themas* are semantically or conceptually connected and co-occurring but are not hierarchically related, KOS may explicitly indicate and link them as associative relationships. Different indicators or labels are used to differentiate that kind of relationships from hierarchical relationships.

Associative relationship links are usually established among *thema*s belonging to different hierarchies, or among overlapping *themas* within the same array on a particular level of the hierarchy. Most commonly considered associative relationships fall into the following categories (Lancaster, 1986; NISO, 2005; Aitchison et al., 2000):

ASSOCIATIVE RELATIONSHIPS	EXAMPLES
Cause/Effect	accident/injury
Process/Agent	velocity measurement/speedometer
Action/Product of the action	weaving/cloth
Action/Patient or Target	teaching/student
Concept or Thing/Properties	steel alloy/corrosion resistance
Thing or Action/Counteragent	pest/pesticide
Thing/Its parts (if it does not qualify for the hierarchical whole-part relationship)	car/engine
Raw material/Product	grapes/wine
Action/Property	communication/communication skills
Field of study/Objects or phenomena studied	forestry/forests

The ISO standard listed common associative relationships to be established in thesauri; many are similar to the above list (ISO, 2011, Clause 10.3.3):

- A discipline or field of study and the objects or phenomena studied
- An operation or process and its agent or instrument
- An action and the product of the action
- An action and its recipient or target
- Objects or materials and their defining properties
- An artefact and its parts, if they do not qualify for the hierarchical whole-part relationship
- Concepts linked by causal dependence
- An object or process and its counteragent
- A concept and its unit of measurement
- A compound term and the noun that is its focus, if the two do not have a true hierarchical relationship

In certain implementations, a decision would be made as to whether and which associative relationships should be included and at what level of specificity.

Associative relationships may also be established for the *themas* that have overlapping meanings, such as medicine and drug, boat and ship, and so on.

Implementation-Dependent Relationships

It is important to emphasize that although FRSAD listed selected semantic relationships according to the standards and best practices that have been used in the construction and implementations of KOS, other approaches to differentiate semantic relation types have been used.

The *Unified Medical Language System* (UMLS) classified semantic relationship types into two main groups and a number of subgroups (NLM, 2009, Section 5.4):

- is_a
- associated_with
  - physically_related_to
  - spatially_related_to
  - functionally_related_to
  - temporally_related_to
  - conceptually_related_to

Spatial relationship types in UMLS include:

- spatially_related_to
  - location_of
  - adjacent_to
  - surrounds
  - traverses

Whereas in another case, such relationship types only for geographical regions are identified as (Hill, 1999):

Inherently spatial
> Containment
>
> Overlap
>
> Proximity
>
> Directional

Explicitly stated
> PartOf
>
> AdministrativePartOf
>
> AdministrativePartitionMemberOf
>
> AdministrativeSeatOf
>
> ConventionallyQualifiedBy
>
> SubfeatureOf
>
> GeophysicalPartitionMemberOf
>
> PhysicallyConnectedTo
>
> FlowsInto

These examples illustrate implementation-dependent relationship typing. In recent years we have seen more ontologies developed for a wide range of subject domains and applications. In addition to the relationships defined by FRSAD, implementation-dependent relationships can be defined as needed by any implementation.

Nomen-to-*Nomen* Relationships

One of the basic functions of authority data is to manage equivalent *nomens* that refer to the same *thema*. Works about computers may use these terms to refer to the same thing: *motherboard, mainboard, baseboard, system board, planar board, logic board* (in Apple), *mobo,* and so forth. It is also common to see the whole-part *nomen*-to-*nomen* relationship, especially when precoordination of subject headings is involved. These two major types are included in this section because they cover the common functionality of subject authority systems. Other *nomen*-to-*nomen* relationships may be established in particular implementations to fulfill specific needs of a particular domain.

Equivalence Relationships

Synonyms is a term that is used widely as an alternative term for *equivalents*. However, in a controlled vocabulary, there may be a broader view of equivalence. According to international standards, the equivalence relationships in a monolingual controlled vocabulary can be found in five general situations (ISO, 2011, Clause 8.1; NISO, 2005):

1. The *nomen*s are synonyms.
2. The *nomen*s are near or quasi-synonyms.
3. The *nomen*s have lexical variants.
4. A *nomen* is regarded as unnecessarily specific and it is represented by another *nomen* with broader scope.
5. A *nomen* is regarded as unnecessarily specific, and it is represented by a combination of two or more terms (known as "compound equivalence").

Looking closely we can see that only case 1 (e.g., salt versus sodium chloride, or apartment versus flat) and case 3 (color versus colour) are real synonyms; the rest apply to situations when the *nomens* represent different *themas* (e.g., forest versus woods, wetness versus dryness, system board versus logic board). In these cases equivalence is understood in a more general sense:

Two *nomens* are considered equivalent only if they are appellations of the same *thema* in a controlled vocabulary.

In addition to the equivalence relationship within a KOS, where it represents the relationship between the preferred and all variant *nomens*, the equivalence relationship also exists between *nomens* across different knowledge information systems and in different languages in general: "gold" (the term in English) is equivalent to "zlato" (a term in Slovenian). Both of these are also equivalent to "Au," the chemical symbol. They all represent the same metal. Figures 5.7 through 5.10 give more examples found in authority systems.

Figure 5.9 illustrates the equivalence across KOS, and Figure 5.10 shows the equivalence relationship between the classification notations and related captions.

When needed, the equivalence relationship may be specified further to express the nature of the relationship. Examples of such refinements include:

- replaces/is replaced by

  This relationship can be used to link an earlier name with a later one (for example, "Muhammad Ali" replaces "Cassius Clay"; "integrated plant control" is replaced by "centralized control").

- has acronym/is acronym for

  A relationship is established between the full name and the acronym: "United Nations" has acronym "UN"; "DDC" is an acronym for "Dewey Decimal Classification."

- has abbreviation/is abbreviation of

  This is a more general relationship compared to "has acronym" and connects a full name with any shorter form: "Incorporated" has the abbreviation "Inc."; "hifi" is abbreviation for "high fidelity."

- has transliterated form/is transliteration of

  This relationship is used to connect the same appellation written in different scripts.

- has translation/is translation of

  This is a relationship between equivalent appellations in different languages: "love" has a translation (into French) of "amour"; "mačka" is the (Slovenian) translation of "cat."

- has vernacular form/is vernacular for

  This relationship can be used to connect the lay form to the scientific one: "rubella" has the vernacular form "measles"; "wolf" is the vernacular for "canis lupus."

FIGURE 5.7 An example of equivalent *nomens* in an authority record for a chemical compound (STN Database Summary Sheet: USAN [The *USP Dictionary of U.S. Adopted Names and International Drug Names*], http://www.cas.org/ASSETS/773D56DEC03E4769BF0E1BC206BB371E/usan.pdf, p. 7[3]).

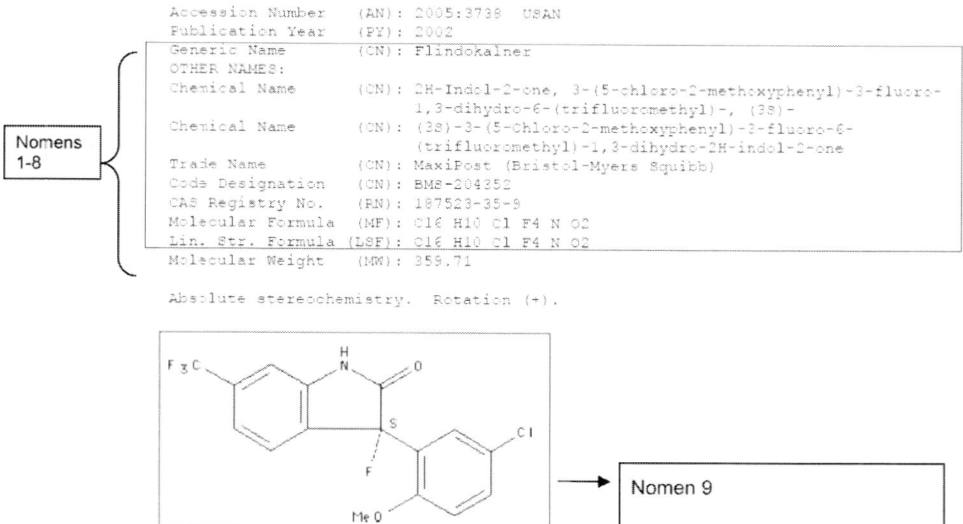

[3] Published with the permission of the US Pharmacopeial Convention and as displayed in STN®, a product of the American Chemical Society (ACS).

FIGURE 5.8 Authority record from LCC.

Schedules Record [LB1032]

ID:CF 94071432 Rec Stat:n Entrd:930207 Used:19960528
CNID:DLC Rec Type:w KOR:a NumType:a Val:a
Opt:a Enc Levl:n Syn:a Dis:a

010 $a CF 94071432
040 $a DLC $c DLC
084 0 $a lcc
153 $a LB1032 $h Theory and practice of education $h Teaching (Principles and practice) $j Group work
553 0 $w I $a LB1140.35.G74 $h Theory and practice of education $h Preschool education. Nursery schools $h Methodology $h Special aspects and methods, A-Z $j Group work in preschool education $t Group work in education
753 $a Group work (Instruction)

Record: 109674
Added: Sun Feb 7 00:00:00 1993
Modified: Tue May 28 10:35:27 1996

Other equivalence relationships may be introduced in particular implementations to reflect specific needs of users or context of the domain.

The Whole-Part Relationship

An instance of a *nomen* may have parts: A personal name is a combination of first name and last name ("Albert Einstein" has parts "Albert" and "Einstein"); a subject heading string is a combination of terms ("Universities and colleges—Employees—Labor unions—Germany"). In such cases a whole-part relationship

FIGURE 5.9 Equivalence of subject headings from different systems as established in MACS. Reprinted with permission from the MACS project.

macs
multilingual access to subjects

Readers
Annotators
Search Links
List Terms
Help
Logout

Editors
Admins
Add New Link
To Do
To Know
Tag Mgt

Supervisors
Maintenance

Searched for **cycling*** in LCSH.
Search retrieved 10 links in 0.67 seconds.

1/1

LCSH	RAMEAU	SWD	Domains	MACS Link	Dups
Cycling **AND** Physiological aspects	--	Radsport **AND** Sportphysiologie	--	MACS0000976	
Cycling	Cyclisme	Radsport	793	MACS0000974	
Cycling	Cyclisme	Radfahren	330 793	MACS0000973	
Cycling accidents	Bicyclettes -- Accidents	Radfahrerunfall	360	MACS0106439	
Cycling accidents	Cyclistes -- Lésions et blessures	Radsport **AND** Sportverletzung	610 793	MACS0000980	
Cycling for women	Cyclisme féminin	Radsport **AND** Frauensport	793	MACS0000981	
Cycling -- Law and legislation	Cyclisme **AND** Droit	Radsport **AND** Sportrecht	340 793	MACS0000975	
Cycling -- Records	Cyclisme **AND** Records	Radsport **AND** Rekord	793	MACS0000977	
Cycling -- Safety measures	Cyclisme **AND** Mesures de sécurité	Radsport **AND** Unfallverhütung	360 793	MACS0000978	
Cycling -- Training	Cyclisme **AND** Entrainement	Radsport **AND** Training	793	MACS0000979	

FIGURE 5.10   A record from LCSH showing variant headings in field 450.

Subject Record [Color blindness]

ID:	sh 85028584	Entered:	860211	Replaced:	19970409
008/06 Geo Subd:	i-Indirect	008/11 SH System:	a-LCSH	008/29 Ref Eval:	a-Eval
008/07 Roman:	I-No attempt	008/15 Subj Use:	a-Appropriate	008/31 Rec Upd:	a-Can be used
008/09 Kind Rec:	a-Estab hdg	008/17 Type Subd:	I-No attempt	008/33 Level Estab:	a-Fully

```
010      $a sh 85028584
040      $a DLC $c DLC $d DLC
053      $a RE921
150  0 $a Color blindness
450  0 $a Achromatism (Disease)
450  0 $a Achromatopic
450  0 $a Achromatopsia
450  0 $a Color vision defects
450  0 $a Color vision disorders
450  0 $a Monochromatism
550  0 $w g $a Vision disorders
670      $a Dorland's med. dict. $b (Monochromatism: also called achromatism, achromatopia, and achromatopsia)
670      $a New York Review of Books, March 6, 1997: $b v. XLIV, no. 4, p. 15 (achromatopsia (complete color blindness))
670      $a MESH $b (Color vision defects X Color blindness)
```

(partial relationship) exists between the *nomen* and its components. In a particular KOS, rules are established to govern the creation of complex *nomens* from such components; for example, the order is determined as well any limitations of what the components can be. Another example is the rules governing the order of facets in a faceted classification system.

ATTRIBUTES

Note: Attributes are underlined in this section to distinguish them from other content.

Thema Attributes

In the FRSAD model, the entity *thema* is defined in a very abstract and general way and covers anything that can be the subject of a work. Therefore attributes of a *thema* are implementation dependent and will vary considerably in different implementations. There are only two attributes applicable in all cases: *type of thema* and *scope note*. All other attributes depend on the particular type a *thema* belongs to.

Type of thema

Definition: The category to which a *thema* belongs in the context of a particular KOS.

In most implementations *themas* will be organized based on category, kind, or type. Relationships within the system and other attributes will depend on *thema* types. Two examples of *thema* types are listed below.

1. UMLS semantic types (NLM, 2003–)

   Entities

   Physical Object

      Organism

      Anatomical Structure

      Manufactured Object

      Substance

   Conceptual Entity

      Idea or Concept

      Finding

      Organism Attribute

      Intellectual Product

      Language

      Occupation or Discipline

      Organization

      Group Attribute

      Group

   Events

      Activity

      Phenomenon or Process

2. AAT facets (AAT, 2000–)

   [Top of the AAT hierarchies]

   Associated Concepts

   Physical Attributes

   Styles and Periods

   Agents

   Activities

   Materials

   Objects

These examples show very different approaches to defining types of *themas*. In the UMLS, *themas* are first differentiated as "Entity" or "Event." The types of UMLS "Entity" are "Physical Object" or "Conceptual Entity." The types of "Events" are grouped into "Activity" and "Phenomenon or Process." In AAT, all *themas* are categorized into seven types: "Associated Concepts," "Physical Attributes," "Styles and Periods," "Agents," "Activities," "Materials," and "Objects."

Clearly, because *themas* are very different, they will also necessarily have different attributes. In the first example, "Organism" will have very different attributes from "Activity" in the UMLS. The same is true for the attributes of "Styles and Periods," "Agents," and "Materials" in AAT.

According to FRBR, *thema* types include *work, expression, manifestation, item, person, corporate body, object, concept, event,* and *place*. Attributes for each of these *thema* types are also specified. While the FRSAD model does not recognize these *thema* types to be universal and generally useful, there may be chosen in some implementations. In these cases FRBR attributes should be consulted.

There are many different ways of classifying *themas*, and for each KOS the choice should be the result of a thorough analysis and an informed decision.

Scope Note

Definition: A text describing and/or defining the *thema* or specifying its scope within the particular subject authority system.

A scope note is often given to a *thema* that is included in KOS to help the users understand the domain. This attribute is particularly important for the *explore* user task.

Nomen **Attributes**

The list of *nomen* attributes below represents only the most common (general) attributes and therefore is not a comprehensive list. Not all listed attributes are applicable to all *nomens*. While the listed attributes are applicable to individual instances of *nomens*, some may also be applied to an entire subject authority system and can be specified on that level.

No attribute values are specified or prescribed, and the examples of attribute values listed below are illustrative only and should not be seen as prescriptive. They only help the understanding of the attributes.

In any particular implementation the actual values of an attribute may come from a controlled list or may be coded.

Current subject authority records typically include other elements such as administrative data. Also, a current authority system may allow merging data —which describe both *thema(s)* and *nomen(s)*—into one record. As this is a conceptual model, such implementation aspects are not discussed.

In the examples below instances of *nomens* are written in brackets (<. . .>) and attribute values are given in quotes (". . .").

Type of nomen

Definition: Category to which the *nomen* belongs.

For each implementation, specific types of *nomens* may be chosen. In general any of the *nomen* attributes may be the basis of different types.

There may be some generally applicable types, particularly:

- "identifier"—the name assigned to an entity that is persistent and unique within a domain
- "controlled name"—the name constructed during the authority control or vocabulary maintenance process that usually serves as an access point (note: labeled as *controlled access point* in FRAD).

The "identifier" type may be further refined to include the particular kind or format of identifier if needed, for example "ISBN" or "URI."

In controlled vocabularies additional types may be specified, such as "preferred form," "variant form," or "non-preferred form."

Examples:

For *nomen* <025.04> the value of type of *nomen* attribute could be "notation"; for *nomen* <Flindokalner> the value could be "generic name."

Scheme

Definition: The scheme in which the *nomen* is established, including value encoding schemes (particular subject heading lists, thesauri, classification systems, name authority lists, etc.) and syntax encoding schemes (standards for encoding dates, etc.).

Examples of attribute values:

- LCSH
- UDC
- ULAN
- ISO 8601

Within one KOS this attribute will apply to all *nomens* included. It is only when several vocabularies are merged that this attribute is applicable to individual *nomens*.

Examples:

For *nomen* <Color blindness>, the value of scheme attribute is "LCSH"; for *nomen* <025.04> the value is "DDC."

Reference source of nomen

Definition: The source in which the *nomen* is found. It may also be modeled as a relationship with the appropriate Group 1 entity (*work*, *expression*, *manifestation*).

Examples of attribute values:

- Encyclopaedia Britannica
- Webster's Third New International Dictionary (1961)
- Columbia Gazetteer

While not important for the end user, this attribute is often included in authority data to support the maintenance and development of a controlled vocabulary.

Example:

An extract from an LCSH record shows "Fletcher, S. E-Mail: a love story, 1996" as reference source of *nomen* <Electronic mail messages>. Additional sources are listed in field 670.

150	0	$a Electronic mail messages 4
450	0	$a E-mail correspondence
450	0	$a E-mail messages
450	0	$a Email correspondence
450	0	$a Email messages
550	0	$w g $a Telematics
670		$a 95-46859: Fletcher, S. E-Mail: a love story, 1996.
670		$a Hennepin $b (E-mail correspondence)
670		$a Crumlish, C. Internet dict., 1995: $b p. 123 (message: an e-mail letter)
670		$a LC database, 7-11-96 $b (electronic messages, computer messages (in titles about e-mail)
670		$a Acad Am. encyc.: $b v. 5, p. 175 (electronic mail: letters and other written messages sent from one computer to another

Representation of nomen

Definition: The data type in which the *nomen* is expressed.

Examples of values:

- Alphanumeric
- Sound
- Graphic

This attribute is applicable only in systems in which different *nomens* are expressed in different data formats. In addition to the general formats listed in the examples, it may be useful in particular implementations to further specify the format; for example in chemistry to specify the kind of graphic representation of substances.

Examples:

For *nomen* <Color blindness> the representation of *nomen* attribute value is "alphanumeric"; *nomen* <∞> has "symbol" as representation of *nomen* attribute value.

Language of nomen

Definition: The language in which the *nomen* is expressed.

Examples of values:

- Greek
- Chinese
- Slovenian

Examples:

For *nomen* <Color blindness> the value of language of *nomen* attribute is "English"; for *nomen* <Barvna slepota> the attribute value is "Slovenian"; for *nomen* <色盲> the attribute value is "Chinese."

Script of nomen

Definition: The script in which a *nomen* is expressed.

Examples of values:

- Cyrillic
- Thai
- Chinese (Simplified)
- Chinese (Traditional)

Examples:

For *nomen* <Καβάπης, Κωνσταντίνος Πέτρου, 1863-1933> the value of script of *nomen* attribute is "Greek"; for *nomen* <图书馆> the value is "Chinese (Simplified)"; while for *nomen* <圖書館> the value is "Chinese (Traditional)."

Script conversion

Definition: The rule, system, or standard used to render the *nomen* in a different representation.

Examples of values:

- Pinyin
- ISO 3602, 1998, Romanization of Japanese (kana script)

This attribute can be used for both transliteration and transcription.

Examples:

For *nomen* <Kabaphēs, Kōnstantinos Petrou, 1863-1933> the value of script conversion attribute is *"ALA-LC Romanization Tables: Transliteration Schemes for Non-Roman Scripts, "Greek" table."* In most implementations the value would be coded.

Form of nomen

Definition: Any additional information that helps to interpret the *nomen*.

Examples of attribute values:

- Full name
- Abbreviation
- Formula

Examples:

For *nomen* <HIV> the value of form attribute is "acronym" (or an appropriate code); for <C16 H10 C1 F4 N O2> the value is "molecular formula."

Time of validity of nomen

Definition: The time period in which a particular instance of a *nomen* is or was used or is or was valid within a subject vocabulary system.

This should not be confused with the temporal aspect of a *thema*. It applies only to the validity of an appellation within a KOS.

Examples of values:

- until May 11, 1949
- after 1945
- 1945–1967

FIGURE 5.11   A record from LCSH stating children as audience.

Subject Record [Belly button]

ID:	sj 96004896	Entered:	960430	Replaced:	19960515
008/06 Geo Subd:	I-No attempt	008/11 SH System:	b-Children	008/29 Ref Eval:	a-Eval
008/07 Roman:	I-No attempt	008/15 Subj Use:	a-Appropriate	008/31 Rec Upd:	a-Can be used
008/09 Kind Rec:	a-Estab hdg	008/17 Type Subd:	I-No attempt	008/33 Level Estab:	a-Fully

```
010    $a sj 96004896
040    $a DLC $c DLC
150  0 $a Belly button
450  0 $a Navel
450  0 $a Umbilicus
```

Examples:

In the *INSPEC Thesaurus*, *nomen* <acoustic surface wave devices> has "Jan 1973 to Jun 1978" as value of time of validity of *nomen* attribute; for *nomen* <acoustic resonance> the value is "from Jan 1978."

Audience

Definition: The community or user group for which this *nomen* is the preferred form.

FIGURE 5.12   A record from LCSH showing the status of variant heading in field 450.

```
000 01709cz a2200361n 450
001 4730870
005 20050804235715.0
008 860211il anannbabn |a ana
035 __ |a (DLC)sh 85080292
035 __ |a (DLC)6567221
035 __ |a (DLC)sp 85080292
035 __ |a (DLC)330487
906 __ |t 0530 |u te04 |v 0
010 __ |a sh 85080292
040 __ |a DLC |c DLC |d DLC |d WaU
150 __ |a Human beings
450 __ |a Homo sapiens
450 __ |a Human race
450 __ |a Humanity (Human beings)
450 __ |a Humankind
450 __ |a Humans
450 __ |w nne |a Man
450 __ |a Mankind
450 __ |a People
550 __ |w g |a Hominids
550 __ |a Persons
670 __ |a Acad. Am. encyc., 1994.
670 __ |a Britannica Micro.
670 __ |a Americana.
670 __ |a Merriam-Web. online dict., June 20, 2005 |b (people: 1 plural : human beings making up a group or assembly or linked by a common
       interest; 2 plural : HUMAN BEINGS, PERSONS -- often used in compounds instead of persons <salespeople>; 3 plural : the members of a family
       or kinship; 4 plural : the mass of a community as distinguished from a special class <disputes between the people and the nobles> -- often used
       by Communists to distinguish Communists from other people; 5 plural peoples : a body of persons that are united by a common culture,
       tradition, or sense of kinship, that typically have common language, institutions, and beliefs, and that often constitute a politically organized
       group)
680 __ |i Here are entered works, primarily of an anthropological nature, on humanity in the collective sense. General works on human beings as
       individuals are entered under |a Persons.
681 __ |i Note under |a Persons
```

In the global environment it is usually impossible to declare one *nomen* of a *thema* to be the preferred form. The notion of preferred form can, in general, be tied only to a particular community, defined by name, rule, or convention.

Examples of values:

- English-speaking users
- Scientists
- Children

Example:

In the subject authority record from LCSH, "Children" is assigned as audience attribute value to *nomen* <Belly button> (Figure 5.11).

Status of a nomen

Definition: The status of a particular *nomen* in a subject authority system.

This should not be confused with the management of a subject authority system (e.g., including or excluding a *thema*).

Examples:

- Proposed
- Accepted
- Obsolete

In the example of the LCSH authority data (Figure 5.12), the *nomen* "Man" is indicated with an <e> as a value for the attribute *status of nomen*. In a MARC record, field 450 $w position /2 value "e" is for "e - Earlier established form of heading."

REFERENCES

Aitchison, J., Gilchrist, A. and Bawden, D. (2000). *Thesaurus Construction and Use: A Practical Manual*, 4th ed. London: Fitzroy Dearborn.

Art and Architecture Thesaurus (AAT) (2000–). Los Angeles: J. Paul Getty Trust, Vocabulary Program. Available at http://www.getty.edu/research/ conducting_research/vocabularies/aat/ (accessed January 20, 2010). Hierarchy Display available at http://www.getty.edu/vow/AATHierarchy ?find=&logic=AND¬e=&english=N&subjectid=300000000 (accessed January 20, 2010).

Campbell, K. E., Oliver, D. E., Spackman, K. A. and Shortliffe, E. H. (1998). "Representing Thoughts, Words, and Things in the UMLS." *Journal of the American Medical Informatics Association* 5 (5): 421–31.

Clarke, S. G. (2001). "Thesaural relationships." In *Relationships in Knowledge Organization*, edited by C. A. Bean and R. Green. Dordrecht: Kluwer.

Dahlberg, I. (1992). "Knowledge Organization and Terminology: Philosophical and Linguistic Bases." *International Classification* 19 (2): 65–71.

Delsey, T. (2005). "Modeling Subject Access: Extending the FRBR and FRANAR Conceptual Models." *Cataloging & Classification Quarterly* 39 (3/4): 49–61.

Encyclopaedia Britannica. Available at; http://www.britannica.com/ (accessed July 10, 2011)

Functional Requirements for Authority Data (FRAD). (2009). München: Saur.

Hill, L. (1999). "Content Standards for Digital Gazetteers." Presentation at the JCDL2002 NKOS Workshop "Digital Gazetteers—Integration into Distributed Digital Library Services," July 18, 2002, Portland, Oregon. Available at http://nkos.slis.kent.edu/DL02workshop.htm (accessed January 20, 2010).

ISO (2011). *ISO/CD 25964-1, Information and Documentation—Thesauri and Interoperability with Other Vocabularies—Part 1: Thesauri for Information Retrieval*. ISO/TC 46 / SC 9 ISO 25964 Working Group.

Iyer, Hemalata. (1995). *Classificatory Structures, Concepts, Relations and Representation*. Frankfurt/Main: INDEKS Verlag.

Lancaster, F. W. (1986). *Vocabulary Control for Information Retrieval*, 2nd ed. Arlington, VA: Information Resources Press.

National Library of Medicine (NLM). (2003–). *Unified Medical Language System*. Homepage available at http://www.nlm.nih.gov/research/umls/ (accessed July 25, 2011).

National Library of Medicine (NLM). (2009) *UMLS® Reference Manual*. Available at http://www.ncbi.nlm.nih.gov/books/NBK9676/ (accessed July 25, 2011-07). 5.4 Hierarchies for Semantic Types and Semantic Relations in the Semantic Network. *Current Relations in the Semantic Network* available at http://www.nlm.nih.gov/research/umls/META3_current_relations. html. *Current Semantic Types* available at http://www.nlm.nih.gov/research/ umls/META3_current_semantic_types.html.

NISO. (2005). *Guidelines for the Construction, Format, and Management of Monolingual Controlled Vocabularies*. ANSI/NISO Z39.19-2005. Bethesda, Maryland: NISO Press.

Ogden, C. K., and Richards, I. A. (1923). *The Meaning of Meaning: A Study of the Influence of Language upon Thought and of the Science of Symbolism*. London: Routledge & Kegan Paul.

Svenonius, E. (2000). *The Intellectual Foundation of Information Organization*. Cambridge, MA: MIT Press.

Formal Presentations
of the FRSAD Model

RECAPITULATION OF FRSAD

This section is intended as an overview of FRSAD for implementers or as a quick reference. All essential information is listed, but for explanations, discussion, and examples the readers should consult other appropriate sections.

Thema		
	Type:	Entity
	Definition:	Anything that serves as subject of a *work*
	Attributes:	Type of *thema* The category to which a *thema* belongs in the context of a particular KOS. Scope note A text describing and/or defining the *thema* or specifying its scope within the particular subject authority system.
Nomen		
	Type:	Entity
	Definition:	Any sign or sequence of signs (alphanumeric characters, symbols, sound, etc.) by which a *thema* is known, referred to, or addressed.
	Attributes:	Type of *nomen* (suggested term: typeOfNomen) Category to which the *nomen* belongs. Scheme (suggested term: scheme) The scheme in which the *nomen* is established, including value-encoding schemes (particular subject heading lists, thesauri, classification systems, name authority lists, etc.) and syntax encoding schemes (standards for encoding dates, etc.). Reference source of *nomen* (suggested term: referenceSourceOfNomen) The source in which the *nomen* is found. It may also be modeled as a relationship with the appropriate Group 1 entity (work, expression, manifestation). Representation of *nomen* (suggested term: representationOfNomen) The data type in which the *nomen* is expressed. Language of *nomen* (suggested term: languageOfNomen)

The language in which the *nomen* is expressed.
Script of *nomen* (suggested term: scriptOfNomen)
  The script in which a *nomen* is expressed.
Script conversion (suggested term: scriptConversion)
  The rule, system, or standard used to render the *nomen* in a
  different representation.
Form of *nomen* (suggested term: formOfNomen)
  Any additional information that helps to interpret the *nomen*.
Time of validity of *nomen* (suggested term: timeOfValidityOf-
Nomen)
  The time period, in which a particular instance of a *nomen*
  is/was used or is/was valid within a subject vocabulary system.
Audience (suggested term: audienceOfNomen)
  The community or user group for which this *nomen* is the
  preferred form.
Status of *nomen* (suggested term: statusOfNomen)
  The status of a particular *nomen* in a subject authority system.

Relationships

Work-to-*thema* relationship		
"has as subject" (suggested term: hasAsSubject)		
	Reverse:	"is subject of" (suggested term: isSubjectOf)
	Domain:	*Work*
	Range:	*Thema*
	Cardinality:	Many-to-many
Thema-to-*nomen* relationship		
"has appellation" (suggested term: hasAppellation)		
	Reverse:	"is appellation of" (suggested term: isAppellationOf)
	Domain:	*Thema*
	Range:	*Nomen*
	Cardinality:	Many-to-many
Thema-to-*thema* relationship		
Hierarchical relationship		
"has broader *thema*" (suggested term: hasBroader) =skos:broader		

	Reverse:	"has narrower *thema*"
	Domain:	*Thema*
	Range:	*Thema*
	Cardinality:	Many-to-many
"has narrower *thema*" (suggested term: isNarrowerThan) =skos:narrower		
	Reverse:	"has broader *thema*"
	Domain:	*Thema*
	Range:	*Thema*
	Cardinality:	Many-to-many
Associative relationship		
"has related *thema*" (suggested term: hasRelated) =skos:related		
	Reverse:	"has related *thema*"
	Domain:	*Thema*
	Range:	*Thema*
	Cardinality:	Many-to-many
Nomen-to-*nomen* relationship		
"is equivalent to" (suggested term: isEquivalentTo)		
	Reverse:	"is equivalent to"
	Domain:	*Nomen*
	Range:	*Nomen*
	Cardinality:	Many-to-many
"has part" (suggested term: hasPart)		
	Reverse:	"is part of"
	Domain:	*Nomen*
	Range:	*Nomen*
	Cardinality:	Many-to-many

"is part of" (suggested term: isPartOf)		
	Reverse:	"has part"
	Domain:	*Nomen*
	Range:	*Nomen*
	Cardinality:	Many-to-many

FRSAD IN RDF

The IFLA Namespace Working Group is currently developing representations of FRBR, FRAD, and FRSAD in RDF.

Tasks, entities and properties are declared in the Open Metadata Registry (http://metadataregistry.org). The namespace uses http://iflastandards.info/ns/fr/frbr/frbrer/ as the basis of the uniform resource identifiers (URIs) of each RDF class and property in the model. The namespace follows the wording of FRBR as closely as possible and relies solely on the FRBR, FRAD, and FRSAD final reports as a source of information. At the time of writing, the namespaces were still under development under the auspices of IFLA. Figure 6.1 is an example.

Tasks

Task	URI	Definition
find	.../fr/frsad/ frsadusertask/1001	Find one or more subjects and/or, their appellations, that correspond(s) to the user's stated criteria, using attributes and relationships.
identify	.../fr/frsad/ frsadusertask/1002	Identify a subject and/or its appellation based on its attributes or relationships (i.e., to distinguish between two or more subjects or appellations with similar characteristics and to confirm that the appropriate subject or appellation has been found).
select	.../fr/frsad/ frsadusertask/1003	Select a subject and/or its appellation appropriate to the user's needs (i.e., to choose or reject based on the user's requirements and needs).
explore	.../fr/frsad/ frsadusertask/1004	Explore relationships between subjects and/or their appellations (i.e., to explore relationships in order to understand the structure of a subject domain and its terminology).

FIGURE 6.1   Screen shot of the FRSAD properties registered in the Open Metadata Registry (Open Metadata Registry, http://metadataregistry.org/schemaprop/list/schema_id/26.html.

Element Sets: Show detail for FRSAD model

| Detail | Elements | History | Maintainers |

Label	Type	URI	Status	Updated	Last Updated by	Actions
has type of thema	property	...ns/fr/frsad/P3001	New-Proposed	2010-09-23 13:33	Gordon Dunsire	
has scope note	property	...ns/fr/frsad/P3002	New-Proposed	2010-09-23 13:33	Gordon Dunsire	
has type of nomen	property	...ns/fr/frsad/P3003	New-Proposed	2010-09-23 13:32	Gordon Dunsire	
has scheme	property	...ns/fr/frsad/P3004	New-Proposed	2010-09-23 13:32	Gordon Dunsire	
has reference source of nomen	property	...ns/fr/frsad/P3005	New-Proposed	2010-09-23 13:32	Gordon Dunsire	
has representation of nomen	property	...ns/fr/frsad/P3006	New-Proposed	2010-09-23 13:31	Gordon Dunsire	
has language of nomen	property	...ns/fr/frsad/P3007	New-Proposed	2010-09-23 13:31	Gordon Dunsire	
has script of nomen	property	...ns/fr/frsad/P3008	New-Proposed	2010-09-23 13:31	Gordon Dunsire	
has script conversion	property	...ns/fr/frsad/P3009	New-Proposed	2010-09-23 13:30	Gordon Dunsire	
has form of nomen	property	...ns/fr/frsad/P3010	New-Proposed	2010-09-23 13:30	Gordon Dunsire	
has time and validity of nomen	property	...ns/fr/frsad/P3011	New-Proposed	2010-09-23 13:29	Gordon Dunsire	
has audience	property	...ns/fr/frsad/P3012	New-Proposed	2010-09-23 13:29	Gordon Dunsire	
has status of nomen	property	...ns/fr/frsad/P3013	New-Proposed	2010-09-23 13:29	Gordon Dunsire	
has as subject	property	...ns/fr/frsad/P2001	New-Proposed	2010-09-23 13:28	Gordon Dunsire	
is subject of	property	...ns/fr/frsad/P2002	New-Proposed	2010-09-23 13:28	Gordon Dunsire	
has appellation	property	...ns/fr/frsad/P2003	New-Proposed	2010-09-23 13:28	Gordon Dunsire	
is appellation of	property	...ns/fr/frsad/P2004	New-Proposed	2010-09-23 13:27	Gordon Dunsire	
Thema	class	...ns/fr/frsad/C1001	New-Proposed	2010-09-23 13:26	Gordon Dunsire	
Nomen	class	...ns/fr/frsad/C1002	New-Proposed	2010-09-23 13:26	Gordon Dunsire	

19 results

Classes

Class	URI	Definition
Thema	http://iflastandards.info/ns/fr/frsad/C1001	Any entity used as a subject of a work.
Nomen	http://iflastandards.info/ns/fr/frsad/C1002	Any sign or sequence of signs (alphanumeric characters, symbols, sound, etc.) by which a *thema* (any entity used as a subject of a work) is known, referred to, or addressed.

Properties

Property Name	URI	Definition	Domain	Range
hasAsSubject	.../ns/fr/frsad/P2001	Relates a *work* to a *thema*.		../ns/fr/frsad/C1001
isSubjectOf	.../ns/fr/frsad/P2002	Relates a *thema* to a *work*.	../ns/fr/frsad/C1001	
hasAppellation	.../ns/fr/frsad/P2003	Relates a *thema* to a *nomen*.	.../ns/fr/frsad/C1001	.../ns/fr/frsad/C1002
isAppellationOf	../ns/fr/frsad/P2004	Relates a *nomen* to a *thema*.	../ns/fr/frsad/C1002	../ns/fr/frsad/C1001

hasType OfThema	../ns/fr/frsad/ P3001	Relates a *thema* to the category to which it belongs in the context of a particular KOS.	../ns/fr/frsad/ C1001	
hasScopeNote	../ns/fr/frsad/ P3002	Relates a *thema* to a text describing and/ or defining the *thema* or specifying its scope within the particular subject authority system.	../ns/fr/frsad/ C1001	
hasTypeOf Nomen	../ns/fr/frsad/ P3003	Relates a *nomen* to a category to which it belongs.	../ns/fr/frsad/ C1002	
hasScheme	../ns/fr/frsad/ P3004	Relates a *nomen* to the scheme in which it is established.	../ns/fr/frsad/ C1002	
hasReference SourceOf Nomen	../ns/fr/frsad/ P3005	Relates a *nomen* to the source in which it is found.	../ns/fr/frsad/ C1002	
has Representation OfNomen	../ns/fr/frsad/ P3006	Relates a *nomen* to the data type in which it is expressed.	../ns/fr/frsad/ C1002	
language OfNomen	../ns/fr/frsad/ P3007	Relates a *nomen* to the language in which it is expressed.	../ns/fr/frsad/ C1002	
scriptOfNomen	../ns/fr/frsad/ P3008	Relates a *nomen* to the script in which it is expressed.	../ns/fr/frsad/ C1002	
hasScript Conversion	../ns/fr/frsad/ P3009	Relates a *nomen* to the rule, system, or standard used to render it in a different representation.	../ns/fr/frsad/ C1002	

hasFormOf Nomen	../ns/fr/frsad/ P3010	Relates a *nomen* to any additional information that helps to interpret it.	../ns/fr/frsad/ C1002	
hasTime OfValidity OfNomen	../ns/fr/frsad/ P3011	Relates a *nomen* to the time period in which it is or was used or is or was valid within a subject vocabulary system.	../ns/fr/frsad/ C1002	
hasAudience	../ns/fr/frsad/ P3012	Relates a *nomen* to the community or user group for which the *nomen* is the preferred form.	../ns/fr/frsad/ C1002	
hasStatus OfNomen	../ns/fr/frsad/ P3013	Relates a *nomen* to its status in a subject authority system.	../ns/fr/frsad/ C1002	

REFERENCES

Functional Requirements for Subject Authority Data: A Conceptual Model (FRSAD). (2010). IFLA Working Group on Functional Requirements for Subject Authority Records (FRSAR). Eds. M. Zeng, M. Žumer, and A. Salaba. Berlin/München: De Gruyter Saur.
Open Metadata Registry. Available at http://metadataregistry.org/ (Accessed July 26, 2011).

CHAPTER 7

Examples of Subject Authority Data Explained with the FRSAD Model

This chapter starts with the interpretation of some basic units in existing KOS where, for the management purpose, subject data are wrapped as "records" or "entries" with human-understandable format. We use the concept of "knowledge organization systems" because it covers more types of structures than the common sense "subject authority files." Following this section are analytical views of FRSAD elements in terms of entity types, attributes, and relationships.

The chapter is written for the purpose of demonstrating the foundation of FRSAD elements and model. Types of KOS and selected examples do not convey any inclusive or exclusive decisions. There are a variety of different micro- and macro-structures in KOS, and this chapter does not attempt to cover all of them. Examples included in this section are selected based on their fundamental structures, presented from simpler to more complex structures.

The convention used in the examples follow what has been presented in Chapter 6. *Nomens* are included in angle brackets <...>, for example: *nomen* <Grayscale>. Attribute values are in quotation marks; they are presented after the equal sign of the attribute's label. For example:

statusOfNomen = "Published".

The syntax used by this chapter is not an encoding recommendation. It is used to show the examples in this book in a consistent format.

EXAMPLES OF DISPLAY RECORDS FROM KNOWLEDGE ORGANIZATION SYSTEMS

Example: A *Thema* and Its *Nomens* in a Simple Controlled List from the *PBCore instantiationColors*

This Example is a value list defined by the *PBCore Public Broadcasting Metadata Dictionary*. A value list is a limited set of terms arranged as a simple alphabetical list or in some other logically evident way such as chronological or numerical order. They are also referred to as "controlled lists" or as the minimum-level "controlled vocabularies." In a simple list, the basic function is to disambiguate

FIGURE 7.1   List view of the *PBCore instantiationColors* vocabulary registered at Open Metadata Registry, URI: http://pbcore.org/vocabularies/instantiationColors. (Open Metadata Registry, http://metadataregistry.org/concept/list/vocabulary_id/134.html).

Vocabulary: Show detail for PBCore instantiationColors

Detail	Concepts	History	Versions	Maintainers

Preferred Label	URI	Status	Updated
B&W	.../instantiationColors#b-w	Published	2011-01-28 10:58
Color	.../instantiationColors#color	Published	2011-01-28 10:58
Grayscale	.../instantiationColors#grayscale	Published	2011-01-28 10:58
Tinted	.../instantiationColors#tinted	Published	2011-01-28 10:58
Toned	.../instantiationColors#toned	Published	2011-01-28 10:58

the meanings of the concepts included. Usually no hierarchical relationships and associative relationships are presented for concepts. It is very straightforward that any *thema* will be represented by its *nomen(s)*.

The screenshots (Figures 7.1 and 7.2) are from the Open Metadata Registry with both the list view and record view. The *PBCore instantiationColors* owner is PBCore, WGBH Educational Foundation.

Behind each preferred label is the concept the label represents. In this screen shot, five *themas* (i.e., concepts) are represented by five *nomens* that were chosen as preferred labels (i.e., typeOfNomen = "preferredForm"). Tacking the third one, the concept that has a preferred label <Grayscale> and a unique URI, has the status "published" and was updated on "2011-01-28."

Figure 7.2 is a detailed view of each concept. Again, taking <Grayscale> as an example, the thema has two *nomens*: <Grayscale> (in English) and <http://

FIGURE 7.2   Record view of a *PBCore instantiationColors* vocabulary concept registered at Open Metadata Registry. (Open Metadata Registry, http://metadataregistry.org/concept/show/id/1482.html>).

pbcore.org/vocabularies/instantiationColors#grayscale>. These two *nomen* types include preferred form and URI (or identifier). Hence the values for the typeOfNomen attribute would be "preferredForm" and "URI" in the following example. A *nomen* also has other attributes (and values) such as languageOfNomen ("English"), statusOfNomen ("Published"), and timeOfValidityOfNomen ("since 2011-01-28"). The attribute scheme ("PBCore instantiationColors") would apply to all *nomens* of this list.

In a structured way, the *nomens* can be explained as:

themaA

    hasAppellation nomen1, nomen2

        nomen1 <Grayscale>

            typeOfNomen = "preferredForm"; languageOfNomen = "English"; scheme = *"PBCore instantiationColors"*; statusOfNomen = "Published"; timeOfValidityOfNomen = "since 2011-01-28".

          nomen2 <http://pbcore.org/vocabularies/instantiationColors#grayscale>

            typeOfNomen = "URI"; statusOfNomen = "Published"; timeOfValidityOfNomen = "since 2011-01-28".

Example: A Chemical Substance and Its *Nomens*—A Display Record from the *USP Dictionary of U.S. Adopted Names and International Drug Names* (USAN)

Figure 7.3 demonstrates how a *thema* can have various *nomens* coming from specific naming systems. The forms of the *nomens* for this chemical compound are not only various names represented in natural language but also those represented in artificial languages such as codes, formulas, and a graph.

In this record, the *thema* has several *nomens*, explained below. The *nomen* has a number of different values for the <u>typeOfNomen</u> attribute and several other attributes such as <u>formOfNomen</u> and <u>representationOfNomen</u>. The *nomen* types are different from the example given in the previous PBCore record. They are obviously shown in the record already, such as "generic name," "chemical name," "trade name," "code designation," "CAS Registry No," "structure formula," and "absolute stereochemistry." The formOfNomen attribute would be very useful to indicate those that are "formula" and "structure," while the representationOfNomen attribute value "graphic" distinguishes the last *nomen* from the others.

Take the first line in the box: this *nomen* <Flindokalner> may be explained as

nomen <Flindokalner>

    typeOfNomen = "generic name"; languageOfNomen = "US Adopted Name"; scheme = "USAN"; timeOfValidityOfNomen = "since 2002".

FIGURE 7.3   A chemical substance record that demonstrates how a *thema* can have various *nomens* from specific naming systems. (Record is from STN Database Summary Sheet: USAN [The USP Dictionary of U.S. Adopted Names and International Drug Names]. http://www.cas.org/ASSETS/773D56DEC03E4769BF0E1BC206BB 371E/usan.pdf, p. 7.[1])

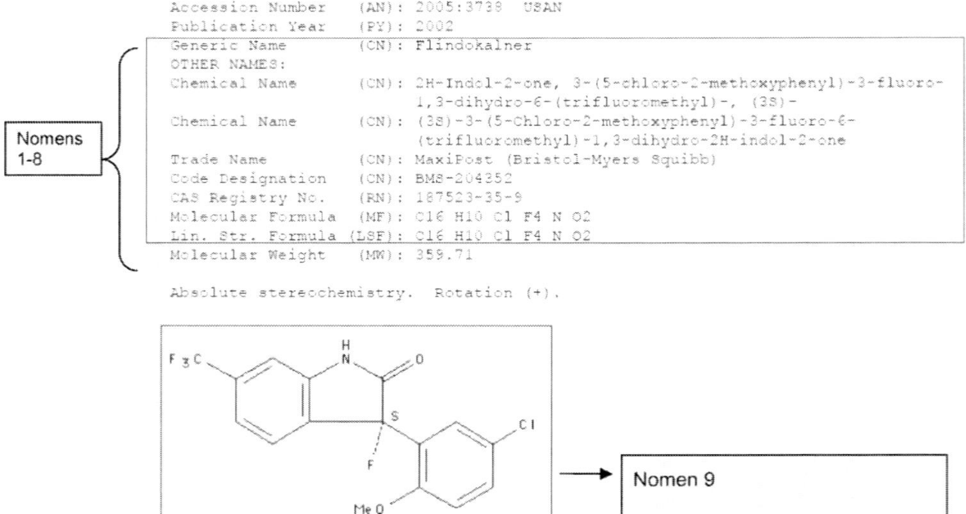

The last line in the box carries a *nomen*, <C16 H10 Cl F4 N O2>, and may be explained as

nomen <C16 H10 Cl F4 N O2>

> typeOfNomen = "linear structure formula"; formOfNomen = "formula"; scheme = "USAN"; timeOfValidityOfNomen = "since 2002".

There is another very special *nomen*: the ring structure. In the search systems for chemical compound information, the ring system and the graphical representation have been unique access points provided by systems. This *nomen* can be explained as

nomen

typeOfNomen = "Absolute stereochemistry"; representationOfNomen = "graphic"; formOfNomen = "structure"; scheme = "USAN"; timeOfValidityOfNomen = "since 2002".

Example: A Place as a *Thema*—A Display Record from the *Getty Thesaurus of Geographic Names* (TGN)

The next example is taken from the *Getty Thesaurus of Geographic Names* (TGN). In this example, a place is a *thema*. Information provided for the *thema* includes names that have been used by different language speakers in different time periods, hierarchical relationships of this place with other places, and *thema* types (Figure 7.4).

Using FRSAD terminology, the record can be explained as:

(1) The *thema* has its unique *nomen*: <ID:7011179>. It is one of the *nomens* used to manage the records. Using this *nomen*, the administrator and other

FIGURE 7.4 A display record in which a place is a *thema*, from TGN (*Source:* © J. Paul Getty Trust. Getty Vocabulary Program. *Getty Thesaurus of Geographic Names* (TGN). Los Angeles: J. Paul Getty Trust. Getty Vocabulary Program, 1988–, http://www.getty.edu/research/tools/vocabularies/tgn/, accessed October 3, 2011. Record reprinted with permission.)

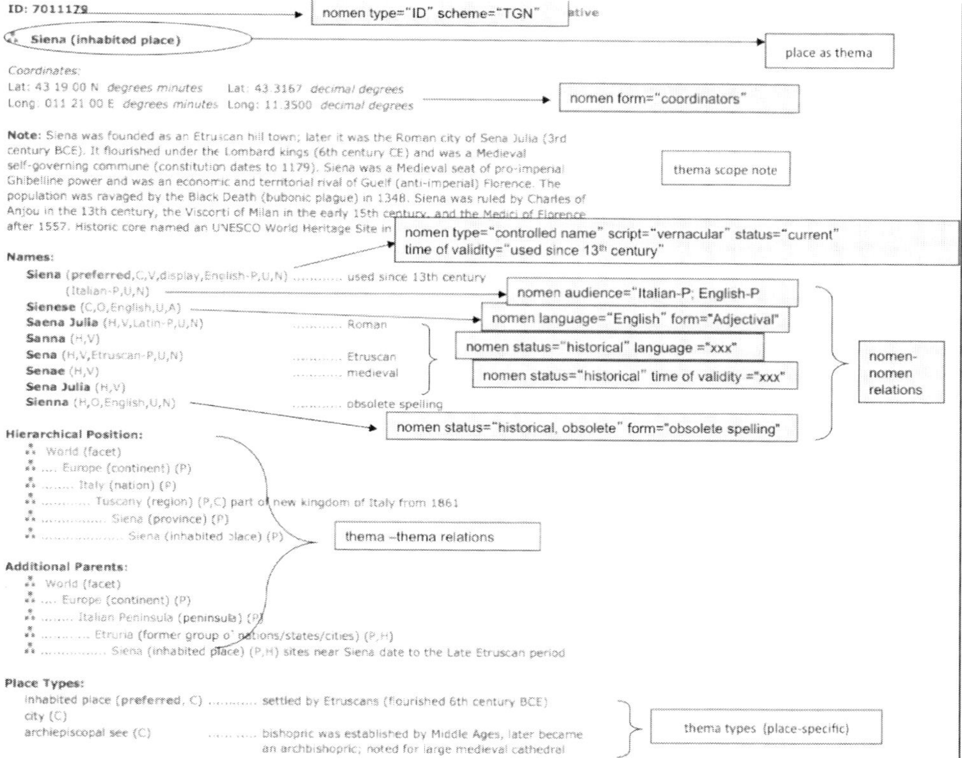

management users will be able to identify the record about this place, as documented in this scheme.

nomen <ID: 7011179>

typeOfNomen = "ID"; scheme = "TGN".

(2) There are other *nomens* that have their literal forms defined in the thesaurus. They are ready to be chosen as preferred terms in different contexts, using information regarding the form, time of validity, status, audience, and source of a particular *nomen*. Here are a few selected examples. (Flags for the *nomens* are explained by TGN as: C = Current; H = Historical; B = Both current and historical; U = Unknown; NA = Not Applicable).

The first line listed under "Names" is

Siena (preferred,C,V,display,English-P,U,N) . . . . used since 13th century

and can be explained as:

The *noman* <Siena> is a preferred local name and it is used since the 13th century.

This *nomen*, <Siena>, has 10 reference sources, all cited in the record.

In a structured presentation we can summarize the attributes and values of this *nomen* as

nomen <Siena>

typeOfNomen = "preferredForm"; audienceOfNomen = "local";
scriptOfNomen = "vernacular"; statusOfNomen = "current";
timeOfValidityOfNomen ="since 13th century";
referenceSourceofNomen = "Annuario Generale (1980);
Canby, Historic Places (1984) 2:861;
Encyclopaedia Britannica Online (1994–2002); . . . .

There are usually different preferred *nomens* in different languages, such as <Saena Julia> for Latin. *Nomen*'s attributes audienceOfNomen and languageOfNomen would be useful to be revealed in various culture- or language-based contexts. For example,

nomen <Saena Julia>

typeOfNomen = "preferredForm"; languageOfNomen = "Latin";
referenceSourceofNomen = "Toscana (non compresa Firenze). Guida d'Italia delTouring Club Italiano. Milano: Touring Club Italiano, 1984. 479".

Historical names including <Sanna>, <Sena>, <Senae>, <Sena Julia>, and <Sienna> are all indicated with a "historical" flag H, and time periods of validity are provided when applicable. Attributes of *nomens* defined by FRSAD such as typeOfNomen (for their non-preferred status in this scheme), timeOfValidity, formOfNomen (e.g., obsolete spelling), and referenceSourceOfNomen would be applied.

(3) The record shows the hierarchical relationships of this inhabited place in relation to its superordinary places in two situations: when the place is regarded as a part of the Siena province in the Tuscany region in Italy, and when the place is considered to belong to Etruria (former group of nations/states/cities) in the Italian Peninsula. These are the "part-of" relationships between *themas*.

(4) The place has types in this scheme. As explained in Chapter 5, typeOf-Thema is a common attribute for *thema*. The values of a typeOfThema attribute are implementation-specific. Here the *thema* types are place related, for example "inhabited place," "city," "world heritage site," "archiepiscopal see," "commune (administrative)," "courtship," and so forth. Each *thema* also has time stamps that can be indicated with additional *thema* attributes defined for this implementation.

Example: Taxonomy with Notations—An Extracted Section from the GAMS Problem Taxonomy

A taxonomy employs category labels (with or without notations) to represent the categories or classes included. In a taxonomy such as the *Guide to Available Mathematical Software (GAMS) Problem Taxonomy*, each *thema* is represented by its unique notation. For example,

N6 = Sorting

N6a = Internal sorting

N6a1 = Passive internal sorting

N6a1a = Integer in passive internal sorting

When a taxonomy or classification system implements a notation system, the captions associated with a notation may not be equivalent to a descriptor or term in a thesaurus because they could be incomplete. In the example below (Figure 7.5), two captions share the same term "Integer" because they are assumed to be used with their superordinates to represent the *thema* of "integer" in "Passive Internal Sorting" or in "Active Internal Sorting." Notations in taxonomies and classifications are the *nomens* most accurately representing *themas*. Here the notations "N6a1a" or "N6a2a" precisely represent the *themas*.

FIGURE 7.5   Extracted classification entries showing classes in hierarchies, unique notations, and identical captions. (GAMS Problem Taxonomy, http://gams.nist.gov/Taxonomy.html. Reprinted with permission.)

```
N6.        Sorting
N6a.         Internal
N6a1.          Passive (i.e. c
N6a1a.           Integer
N6a1b.           Real
N6a1c.           Character
N6a2.          Active
N6a2a.           Integer
N6a2b.           Real
N6a2c.           Character
N6b.         External
N7.        Merging
N8.        Permuting
```

As indicated in Chapter 5, FRSAD model has defined only general attributes and relationships for *thema* and *nomen* entities. Implementation-specific attributes and relationships can be established according to the need. In this example, captions of classes in a taxonomy are treated as a type of *nomen* (typeOfThema = "caption"), with a special relationship "isCaptionOf" (which is a specialization of the equivalence relationship) with a notation.

Notation <N6a1a> and caption <Sorting/Internal/Active/Integer> are two *nomens*; they both represent the same *thema* in this example.

- ThemaA **hasAppellation** Nomen1 and Nomen2
- ThemaA

    Nomen1 <N6a1a>

    typetypeOfThema = "notation";

    scheme = "GAMS Problem Taxonomy".

    Nomen2 **<Sorting/Internal/Active/Integer>**

    typetypeOfThema = "caption";

    scheme = "GAMS Problem Taxonomy".

- **<Sorting/Internal/Active/Integer> isCaptionOf** <N6a1a>

- <N6a1a> **hasCaption <Sorting/Internal/Active/Integer>**

Classification systems may have much more complicated structures than the example given above. In Chapter 8.1 we give more comparison of classification with other types of KOS.

Example: A Thesaurus Editing Tool View of a Record from the *ASIS&T Thesaurus*

The example (Figure 7.6) is taken from the *ASIS&T Thesaurus* hosted by Access Innovation's Data Harmony® Thesaurus Master® thesaurus editing tool at http://thesview.accessinn.com/asistThes/. On the left side is the typical output of a thesaurus in which all terms are shown. A concept (*thema*) in a thesaurus is represented by a preferred term (*nomen*) and other non-preferred terms (also *nomens*). Semantic relationships between and among concepts are presented using standardized indicators of Broader Term (BT), Narrower Term (NT), and Related Term (RT).

Let's select two *themas* to explore. ThemaA is represented by *nomen* <faceted browsing> and ThemaB is represented by *nomen* <faceted classification>.

On the right side of the editor screen, we see the management side of thesauri. In addition to the relationships mentioned above, there are a <u>scope note</u> for a *thema* and the <u>facet</u> a *thema* belongs to if the vocabulary is a faceted thesaurus. For administrative attributes, there are "editorial note" and "history"; both are associated with the first time a *nomen* is established in this thesaurus.

FIGURE 7.6 Thesaurus entry record as seen by the thesaurus editor. (Screen captured from *ASIS&T Thesaurus*, hosted by Access Innovation's Data Harmony Thesaurus Master thesaurus editor at http://thesview.accessinn.com/asistThes/. Reprinted with permission.).

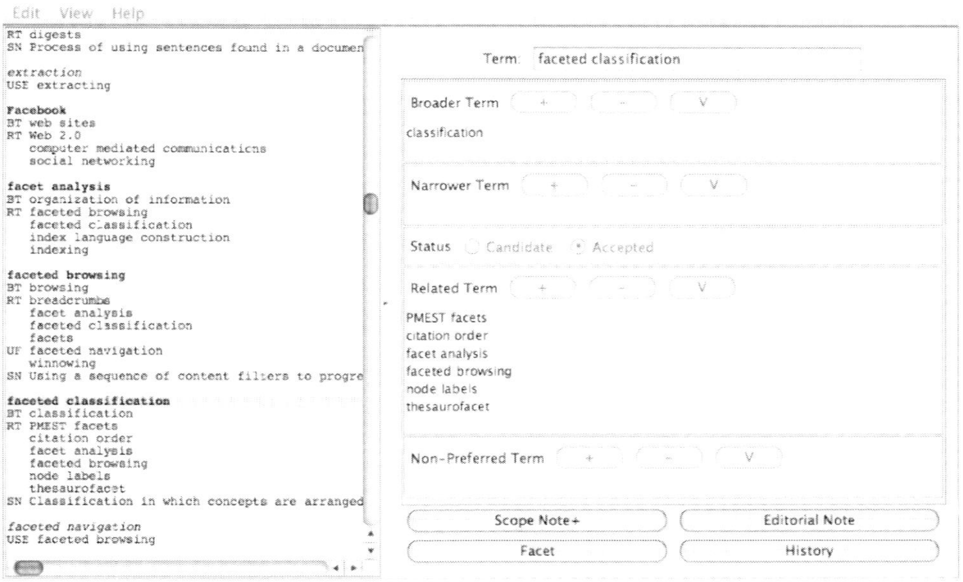

Let's take themaA, which is represented by its *nomen* in preferred form <faceted browsing>. It has two non-preferred *nomens*: <faceted navigation> and <winnowing>. It also has a scope note, "Using a sequence of content filters to progressively narrow a selection set and locate desired content." In a structured format it can be presented as

- themaA
  - **hasApplelation** nomen1, nomen2, nomen3
    - nomen1 <faceted browsing>
      - typeOfNomen = "preferred form".
    - nomen2 <faceted navigation>
      - typeOfNomen = "non-preferred form".
    - nomen3 <winnowing>
      - typeOfNomen = "non-preferred form".
- themaA
  - ScopenoteOfThema = "Using a sequence of content filters to progressively narrow a selection set and locate desired content."

Let's also look at themaB, which is represented by its *nomen* in preferred form <faceted classification>. It has a scope note, "Classification in which concepts are arranged in a series of facets, and the notation for subjects is derived by combining the notations of its individual facets." In a structured format it can be presented as

- themaB
  - **hasApplelation** nomen1
    - nomen1 <faceted classification>
      - typeOfNomen = "preferred form".
- themaB
  - ScopenoteOfThema = "Classification in which concepts are arranged in a series of facets, and the notation for subjects is derived by combining the notations of its individual facets."

The semantic relationship between the two *themas* is "RT," as defined by the thesaurus. The relationships are reciprocal; therefore they can be presented as:

themaA **isRelatedTo** themaB

themaB **isRelatedTo** themaA

There are a number of other semantic relationships between themaA and other *themas*; so also between themaB and other *themas*. (These are not further explained here, though.)

Example: A Multilingual Thesaurus Record from the *Thesaurus Ethics in the Life Sciences*

In this example (Figure 7.7), the *thema* instance has three preferred *nomens* in the respective languages of this thesaurus: "ethics" (English), "Ethik" (German), and "éthique" (French). Non-preferred terms are also in all three languages.

FIGURE 7.7   A multilingual thesaurus record example showing a *thema* instance that has three preferred forms in the respective languages in the thesaurus. (Compiled based on the records in *Thesaurus Ethics in the Life Sciences*, 7th ed.– (December 2010), available at http://www2.drze.de/BELIT/thesaurus/sachgebiete.html?la=en, or ?la=fr, ?la=de Reprinted with permission.)

English	German	French

ethics
Subj. Area:
  I Ethics, Philosophy, Theology
Ger:
  Ethik
Fr:
  éthique
SN:
  Philosophical discipline that seeks the criteria of good human life, action and conduct and that attempts to define it theoretically on the basis of different methods (based on Brockhaus-21); …
UF:
  ethical aspectsethical issuesmoral philosophy
. . . . . .
RT:
  humanities philosophy of law
Conc:
  B: Ethics
  E: ethics
  E: moral philosophy
  I: éthique
  I: philosophie morale
  M: Ethics (D004989)
	Ethik
	Sachgebiet:
	  I Ethik, Philosophie, Theologie
	En:
	  ethics
	Fr:
	  éthique
	SN:
	  Philosophische Disziplin, die nach dem Maß des guten menschlichen Lebens, Handelns und Verhaltens fragt und dieses auf der Grundlage verschiedener Methoden theoretisch zu bestimmen versucht (in Anl. an Brockhaus-21); …
	UF:
	  Ethischer Aspekt
	  Moralphilosophie
	  Sittenlehre
	. . . . . .
	RT:
	  Humanities
	  Rechtsphilosophie
	Konk:
	  B: Ethics
	  E: ethics
	  E: moral philosophy
	  I: éthique
	  I: philosophie morale
	  M: Ethics (D004989)
		éthique
		Champ sémantique:
		  I Éthique, philosophie, théologie
		Ger:
		  Ethik
		En:
		  ethics
		SN:
		  Discipline philosophique qui cherche à établir un système de référence pour une bonne vie, action et conduite humaines età le définir théoriquement en se basant sur différentes méthodes (d'après Brockhaus-21) ; …
		UF:
		  aspect éthique
		  philosophie morale
		. . . . . .
		RT:
		  philosophie du droit
		  sciences humaines
		Conc:
		  B: Ethics
		  E: ethics
		  E: moral philosophy
		  I: éthique
		  I: philosophie morale
		  M: Ethics (D004989)

Indicators:

Subj. Area: subject area(s) in which the descriptor is located

Ger: corresponding descriptor in the German version

Fr: corresponding descriptor in the French version

SN: Scope Note

UF: Used for; indicates that the descriptor has one or more nondescriptors

RT: related term; clickable

Conc: concordances, i.e., the descriptor(s) or descriptor combinations that were used in the reference thesauri in order to express the same concept. [B: Bioethics Thesaurus, E: Euroethics Thesaurus, M: MeSH (in brackets: MeSH Unique Identifier); I: INSERM Thesaurus]

The explanation of this section will focus on the multilingual *nomens* and the mapped concepts in other KOS. The *thema* has 12 *nomens*. There is one preferred form *nomen* in each language: English, German, and French.

- themaA

    hasAppellation nomen1, nomen2, ... nomen12

    noteOfThema = "…" (lang = "…")

    nomen1 <ethics>

      languageOfNomen = "English"; typeOfNomen = "preferred form".

    nomen2 <Ethik>

      languageOfNomen = "German"; typeOfNomen = "preferred form".

    nomen3 <Ethik>

      languageOfNomen = "French"; typeOfNomen = "preferred form".

There are non-preferred *nomens* in each language. The English examples are provided below. The German and French non-preferred forms have the same attributes.

    nomen4 <ethical aspects>

      languageOfNomen = "English"; typeOfNomen = "non-preferred form".

    nomen5 <ethical issues>

      languageOfNomen = "English"; typeOfNomen= "non-preferred form".

    nomen6 <moral philosophy>

      languageOfNomen = "English"; typeOfNomen = "non-preferred form".

Another important feature of this multilingual thesaurus is its concordance component. The concordances provide mapping *themas* in four target reference thesauri. *Nomen*'s attribute <u>scheme</u> is used to indicate where the *nomen* is from. Using the English preferred form of the *nomen* as an example, these will be presented as the following:

- themaA

  hasAppellation nomen1, nomen2, ... nomen12

  Note = "..."

  nomen1 <ethics>

  language = "English"; type = "preferred form";

  scheme = "Thesaurus Ethics in the Life Sciences".

- themaX

  hasAppellation nomen1

  Note = "..."

  nomen1 <Ethics>

  language = "English"; type= "preferred form";

  scheme = "Bioethics Thesaurus".

Now the concordance is expressed through the relationship between the two *themas* and can be coded using skos:closeMatch (more about SKOS [Simple Knowledge Organization System] will be discussed in Chapter 8):

themaA **skos:closeMatch** themaX

Example: A Display Record (Expanded Concept View) from MeSH

Thema-to-*thema* relationships presented in the MeSH's expanded concept view display an important component for "Concept 1: Mercury" (Figure 7.8). The summary of the semantic relationships displayed in this record is presented below the figure.

This expanded concept view presents various types of semantic relationships among *themas*:

- Two immediate hierarchical relationships: (1) between *themas* represented by *nomens* <Mercury> and <Transition Elements>. The same is true for these *themas* and their *nomens* with notational forms; (2) between *themas* represented by the *nomens* <Mercury> and <Metals, Heavy>. The latter can be traced to two upper classes.

- Associative relationships between <Mercury> (as a liquid metal and as an element) and other *themas* represented by *nomens* <Mercury Isotopes>, <Mercury Radioisotopes>, and <Organomercury Compounds>.

- Allowable qualifiers enable the concept to be further limited to specific perspectives (e.g., "administration & dosage [AD]," "isolation & purification [IP]," and "toxicity [TO]"). These facilitate the forming of specific subject headings (e.g., <Mercury – TO>, or <Mercury – IP>) to represent different *themas*.

- The semantic types of this *thema*: <T131 (Hazardous or Poisonous Substance)> and <T196 (Element, Ion, or Isotope)> as defined by UMLS.

FIGURE 7.8   An expanded concept view from MeSH (*Medical Subject Headings* on MeSH Browser [2008 MeSH], National Library of Medicine, http://www.nlm .nih.gov/mesh/2008/MBrowser.html).

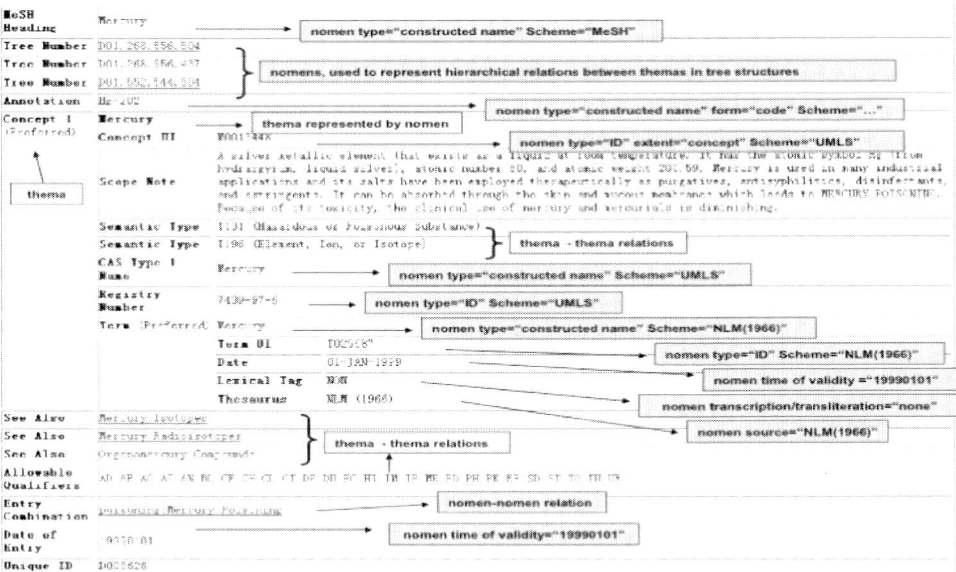

Thema-to-*nomen* relationships are clearly presented in the record, including the *nomens* in natural languages and as specific identification numbers. Various attributes of *nomens* are also presented.

EXPLANATIONS OF FRSAD'S MAJOR COMPONENTS WITH EXAMPLES

This section provides further explanations of FRSAD's major components using the examples found in existing KOS instances. Some of the examples were mentioned in the section "Attributes" (Chapter 5) in relation to attributes of *thema* types. Presented in three parts are: (1) existing models of *thema* types; (2) *thema*-to-*thema* relationships presented in subject authority data (both in individual vocabularies and cross-schemes); and (3) same *thema* represented by *nomens* from different schemes.

Existing Models of *Thema* Types

In Section "*Nomen* Attributes" (Chapter 5), "type" is defined as a general attribute of *thema* because other attributes are usually implementation dependent. In any particular application, *themas* would normally have particular implementation-specific types. Based on our preliminary study, there seems to be no generally applicable categorization of *themas*. This is also supported by the following examples, ranging from general (FAST) to more specialized subject domains such as biomedical and health sciences (UMLS and *Foundational Model of Anatomy* [FMA] ontology) and art and architecture (AAT).

Example: FAST Subject Facets

FAST (Faceted Application of Subject Terminology) (FAST, 2001–) is an adaptation of the LCSH with a simplified syntax. LCSH forms the basis for the FAST authority file. FAST employs a faceted approach by defining headings according to their functions and categorizes all headings into eight facets. Seven of them are subject facets, and one is a form (genre) facet. The subject facets include:

- Topical
- Personal Names (as Subjects)
- Corporate Names (as Subjects)
- Geographics
- Periods
- Titles
- Events

Headings in the FAST database include both single-concept and multiple-concept headings. Each FAST heading or heading string belongs to a single facet.

Example: UMLS Semantic Types

The UMLS, developed, maintained, and distributed by the National Library of Medicine of the United States, provides a unified system for correlating a large number of biomedical terminologies (NLM, 2003–). In order to facilitate the establishment of correspondences in the meanings of terms, the same concepts occurring in different constituent vocabularies are assigned to high-level semantic types encompassed within the *UMLS Semantic Network*. It consists of (1) a set of broad subject categories, or **semantic types**, that provide a consistent categorization of all concepts represented in the *UMLS Metathesaurus*, and (2) a set of useful and important relationships, or **semantic relations**, which exist between semantic types. More than 130 semantic types and 50 semantic relationships defined by the UMLS can be found in the *UMLS Reference Manual* (NLM, 2009). The following are the high-level semantic types:

Entities
    Physical Object
        Organism
        Anatomical Structure
        Manufactured Object
        Substance
    Conceptual Entity
        Idea or Concept
        Finding

Organism Attribute

Intellectual Product

Language

Occupation or Discipline

Organization

Group Attribute

Group

Events

Activity

Phenomenon or Process

The scope of the *UMLS Semantic Network* is broad, allowing for the semantic categorization of a wide range of terminology in multiple domains. The top-level types are **Entities** (including "Physical Object" and "Conceptual Entity") and **Events** (including "Activity" and "Phenomenon or Process"). Looking at its major groupings of semantic types (such as organisms, anatomical structures, biologic function, chemicals, events, physical objects, and concepts or ideas), it is obvious that they are designed to be especially applicable in the biomedical and health areas.

Example: FMA Ontology Semantic Types

FMA (Foundational Model of Anatomy), initially developed as an enhancement of the anatomical content of UMLS, is a domain ontology of the concepts and relationships that pertain to the structural organization of the human body (FMA, 2006). It was found that while there is considerable correspondence in the meaning of anatomical terms in the UMLS sources, there is very little similarity in the arrangement of anatomical terms among the source schemas. It is important that the underlying semantic structure of these abstractions must also be aligned. The top-level semantic types are **Anatomical Entity**, **Attribute Entity**, and **Dimensional Entity**:

Anatomical Entity

Nonphysical anatomical entity

Physical anatomical entity

Attribute Entity

Cell morphology

Cell shape type

Cell surface feature

Concept name

Miscellaneous term

Organ part phenotype

Physical attribute relationship

Physical state

Structural relationship value

Dimensional Entity

Line

Point

Surface

Volume

As a domain ontology, the FMA represents deep knowledge of the structure of the human body. Its emphasis is on the highest level of granularity of the concepts. Meanwhile it also presents a great number of specific structural relationships between the references of these concepts. According to project documentation (FMA, 2006), the FMA consists of approximately 75,000 anatomical classes, 130,000 unique terms, 205,000 frames, and 170 unique slots showing different types of relations, attributes, and attributed relationships. FMA is a typical example of modeling that shows how **semantic types** for a concept scheme can be defined. It not only encompasses the diverse entities that make up the human body but is also capable of modeling a great deal of knowledge relating to these entities.

Example: AAT Facets

The AAT is a controlled vocabulary for fine art, architecture, decorative arts, archival materials, and material culture for the purposes of indexing, cataloging, and searching, as well as a set of research tools. It was developed for literature about art and architecture and for records describing works of art and architecture. The facets in AAT are conceptually organized in a scheme that proceeds from abstract concepts to concrete, physical artifacts. These facets are "Associated Concepts," "Physical Attributes," "Styles and Periods," "Agents," "Activities," "Materials," and "Objects." Homogeneous groupings of terminology, or hierarchies, are arranged within the seven facets of the AAT (AAT, 2000–):

Top of the AAT hierarchies

Associated Concepts Facet

Associated Concepts

Physical Attributes Facet

Attributes and Properties

Conditions and Effects

Design Elements

Color

Styles and Periods Facet

Styles and Periods

Agents Facet

People

Organizations

Living Organisms

Activities Facet

Disciplines

Functions

Events

Physical and Mental Activities

Processes and Techniques

Materials Facet

Materials

Objects Facet

Object Groupings and Systems

Object Genres (Hierarchy Name)

Components (Hierarchy Name)

Built Environment (Hierarchy Name)

Furnishings and Equipment

Visual and Verbal Communication

The conceptual framework of facets is not subject specific. One example is the subject "Renaissance painting." Terms to describe Renaissance paintings will be found in many locations in the AAT hierarchies rather than in a defined portion that is specific only for Renaissance painting (AAT, 2000-, "About the AAT").

In summary, all examples in this section indicate that in actual implementations there are always attempts to define some fundamental facets or atoms to accommodate all types of *themas*. However, the resulting *thema* "types" differ from implementation to implementation.

Thema-to-*Thema* Relationships Presented in Subject Authority Data in Individual Vocabularies

Authority **records** can be stored and displayed differently within a system, and they may also have various combinations of components when displayed to:

- information professionals who create and maintain subject authority data, including cataloguers and controlled vocabulary creators;
- information professionals who create and maintain metadata;

- reference services librarians and other information professionals who search for information as intermediaries; and

- end users who search for information to fulfil their information needs.

Therefore, it is the authority **data**, not the **records**, that will be the focus in the examples presented in the following sections.

The emphasis of this section is on the semantic relations presented in vocabularies. The following examples demonstrate how *thema*-to-*thema* relationships are presented in different vocabularies for the same *thema*, "recycling," and its related *themas* such as "water conservation." The reason for choosing these *themas* was that they are included in all the vocabularies used in this chapter, across a wide range of subject domains.

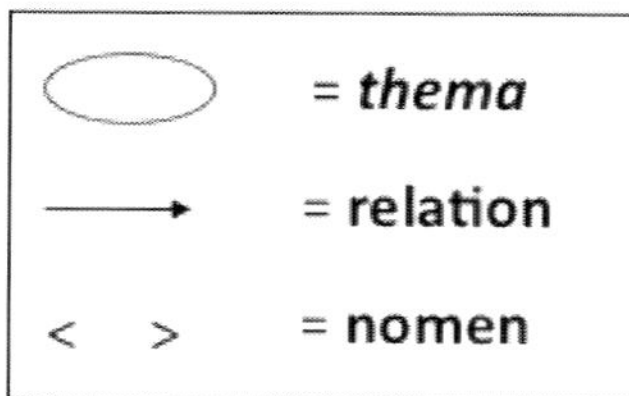

Note: In the figures in this section, an oval-shaped node is used to represent a *thema*. A *nomen* is linked using an arrow to the *thema* it represents and is enclosed in angle brackets.

Example: Data Extracted from an LC Subject Authority Record—Genus-Species Relationship

LC Control Number: sh85145542
150 $a Water conservation
550 $w g $a Conservation of Natural Resources

Note: The MARC21 codings used are:

150 = Heading—Topical term

550 = *See Also* From Tracing—Topical Term;

$a = Topical term or geographic name entry element

$w = Control subfield; g—Broader term

The example shows a hierarchical semantic relationship between the *thema* that has as *nomen* <Water conservation> and another *thema*, which has as *nomen* <Conservation of natural resources>, as illustrated below (Figure 7.9). This relationship can be recognized by the field tag "550," which means "see also," and the value "g" in its controlled subfield $w.

FIGURE 7.9   Illustration of the hierarchical semantic relations between two *themas* represented in an LCSH authority record.

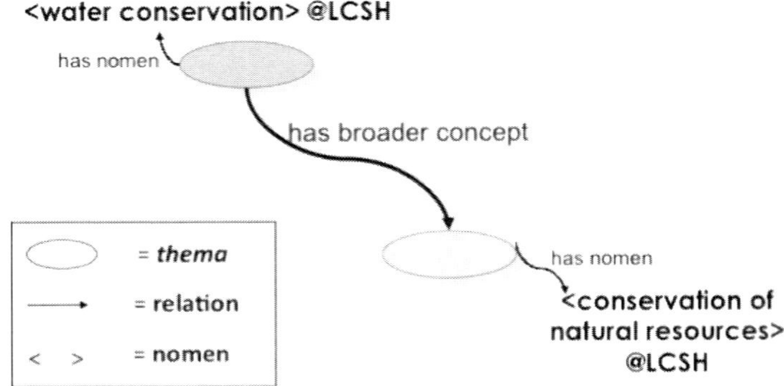

***Example: Data Extracted from AAT—Genus-Species
Relationships, Multiple Levels***

> **ID**: 300191243
> **Preferred term**: *recycling*
> **Hierarchical position**:
>   . <functions by general context>
>   .. maintenance
>   ... waste management
>   .... *recycling*

Note: In this example, hierarchical relationships of the *themas* represented by *nomens* <recycling>, <waste management>, and <maintenance> in three levels are presented in the hierarchy within the facet "functions by general context." Note only the preferred *nomens* are included in the figure (see Figure 7.10).

FIGURE 7.10   Illustration of the semantic relations between three *themas* presented in a concept record in Art and Architecture Thesaurus® Online, http://www.getty.edu/research/tools/vocabularies/aat/index.html.

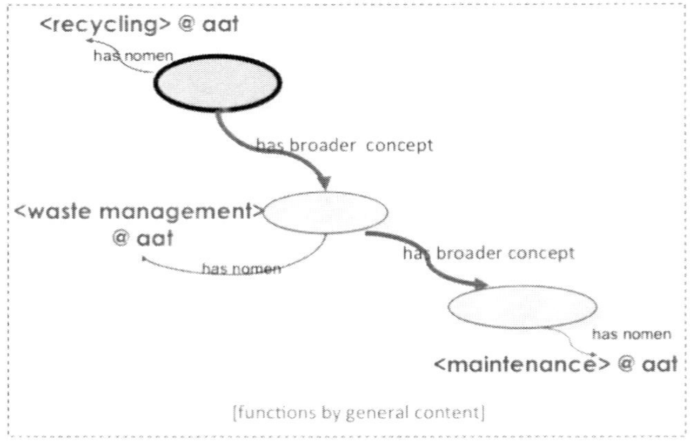

***Example: Data Extracted from an Expanded Concept View in MeSH—
Polyhierarchical and Perspective Relationships***

<table>
<tr><td colspan="2">

Concept UI: M0005042
Term (preferred): <u>Recycling</u>
       Term UI:T009464
Tree Number: J01.256.675
             N06.850.780.200.800.800.525
             N06.850.860.510.244
Allowable qualifiers: EC ES HI LJ MT SN ST TD
MeSH Tree Structures:
</td></tr>
<tr><td>J01</td><td>Technology, Industry, and Agriculture c</td></tr>
<tr><td>J01.256</td><td>. Conservation of Natural Resources</td></tr>
<tr><td><u>J01.256.675</u></td><td>.. <u>Recycling</u></td></tr>
<tr><td>N06</td><td>Environment and Public Health</td></tr>
<tr><td>N06.850.</td><td>. Public Health</td></tr>
<tr><td>N06.850.780</td><td>. . Public Health Practice</td></tr>
<tr><td>N06.850.780.200.800.800</td><td>. . . Sanitary Engineering</td></tr>
<tr><td><u>N06.850.780.200.800.800.525</u></td><td>. . . . <u>Recycling</u></td></tr>
<tr><td>N06</td><td>Environment and Public Health</td></tr>
<tr><td>N06.850.</td><td>. Public Health</td></tr>
<tr><td>N06.850.860.</td><td>. Sanitation</td></tr>
<tr><td>N06.850.860.510</td><td>. . . Sanitary Engineering</td></tr>
<tr><td><u>N06.850.860.510.244</u></td><td>. . . .<u>Recycling</u></td></tr>
</table>

Note: The extracted data is from the expanded concept view of a MeSH record
found through the MeSH Browser, available at http://www.nlm.nih.gov/cgi/
mesh/2011/MB_cgi?mode=&index=26124&view=expanded.

The polyhierarchical relationships can be traced following the tree numbers. Analysis reveals three immediate hierarchical relationships (see the headings and notational forms of *nomens*): (1) between *themas* represented by *nomens*
<Recycling> and <Conservation of Natural Resources>; (2) between *themas*
represented by *nomens* <Recycling> and two <Sanitary Engineering> *nomens*
that have different categorizations (as indicated by their notations and broader
themas).

The allowable qualifiers stand for: EC (economics), ES (ethics), HI (history), LJ (legislation - & jurisprudence), MT (methods), SN (statistics - &
numerical data), ST (standards), and TD (trends). The allowable qualifiers enable the forming of more complex concepts, revealing the particular perspectives of the main *thema*. When used to refine the concept, the aspect of a
concept is indicated clearly; for example, <Recycling – methods>, <Recycling
– Statistics & numerical data>, and many more.

FIGURE 7.11 Illustration of the polyhierarchical relationships (through the tree structure) from the extracted MeSH concept record.

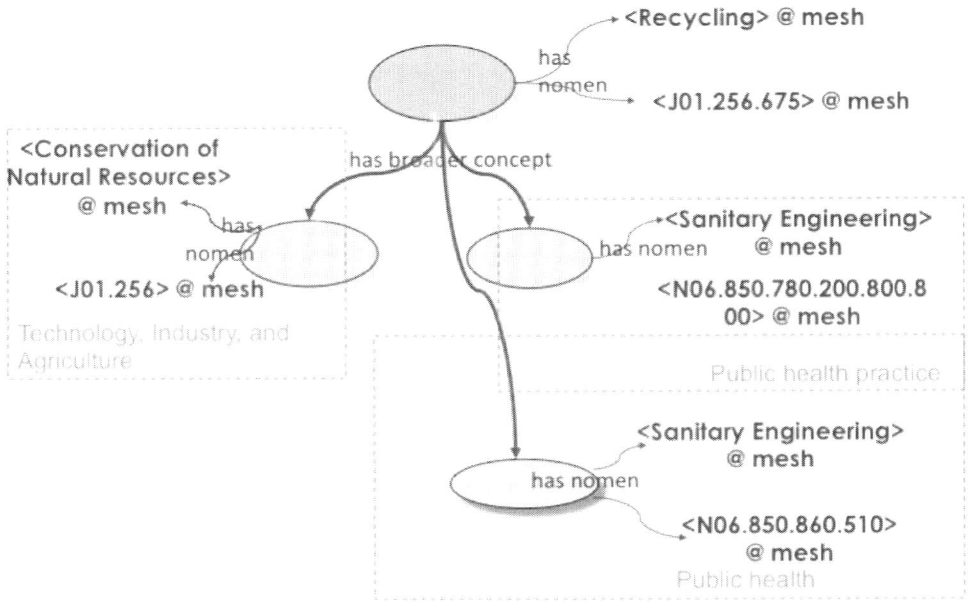

Figure 7.11 only includes immediate upper-level *themas*.

Example: Data Extracted from a Thesaurus Entry in* AGROVOC Thesaurus *Indicating Semantic Relations with Broader, Narrower, and Related Concepts

> *Recycling (6478)*
> BT Waste utilization (16202)
> NT Recycling of drainage water (330871)
> NT Organic recycling (331390)
> RT Pollution control (6078)
> RT Water reuse (36345)

Note: the number ("6478") following the term ("Recycling") is the unique ID of the concept. For details and a full hierarchical display, see http://aims.fao .org/en/agrovoc-term-info?mytermcode=6478&mylang_interface=en&my Language=EN.

The example is taken from the *AGROVOC Thesaurus* of the Food and Agriculture Organization (FAO) of the United Nations. The thesaurus is available in 19 languages as of June 2011. Only the English version is used here. The concept identified by ID 6478 and a preferred *nomen* <Recycling> is presented with its broader concept (BT), narrower concepts (NTs), and related

FIGURE 7.12   Illustration of the hierarchical relationships and associative relationships from the extracted AGROVOC entry.

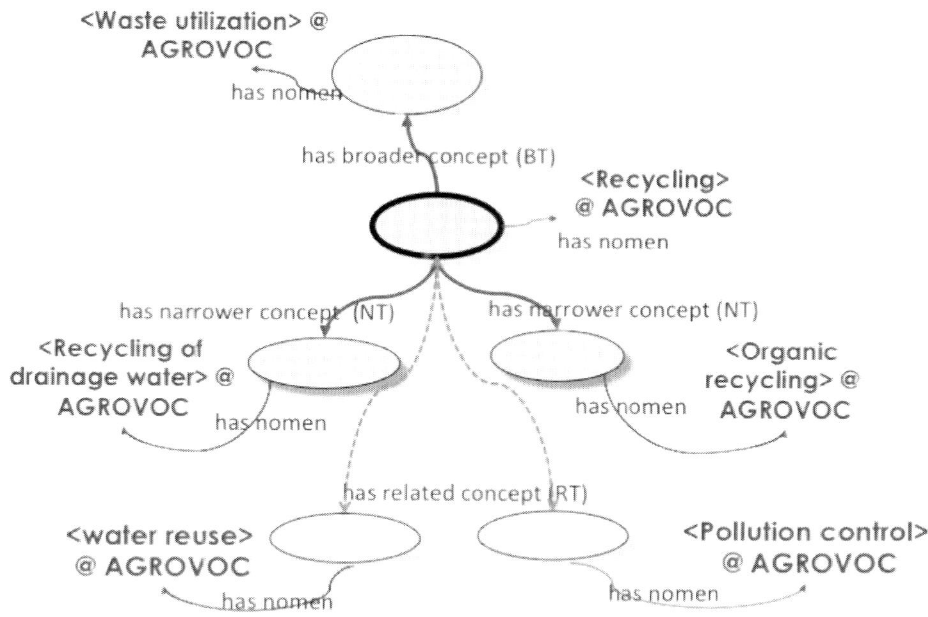

concepts (RTs). The indicators of BT, NT, and RT are defined by international and national thesaurus standards and are used widely. See Figure 7.12.

Example: Extracted Data from a Class in DDC Presenting the Hierarchical Relationships with the Notations

Class Number: *363.7282*
Caption: *Recycling*
[Class position]:

363	Other social problems and services
363.7	Environmental problems
363.72	*Sanitation
363.728	Wastes
363.7282	Recycling

Note: Although in this example the relationships are similar to what is presented in other thesauri (shown previously), in a classification scheme such relationships are presented through the notational codes associated with *themas*, which reflect the conceptual hierarchy of a scheme. Hence it is the **notations** (<669.71> and <546.663>) that are primary *nomens* representing the *themas* (Figure 7.13). If captions are used as a *nomen* (type = "caption"), a full caption with appropriate upper-level captions should be used. (See explanation in Section "Taxonomy with notations—An extracted section from the GAMS Problem Taxonomy.")

FIGURE 7.13   Illustration of the hierarchical relationships (through the classificatory structure) between the DDC classes.

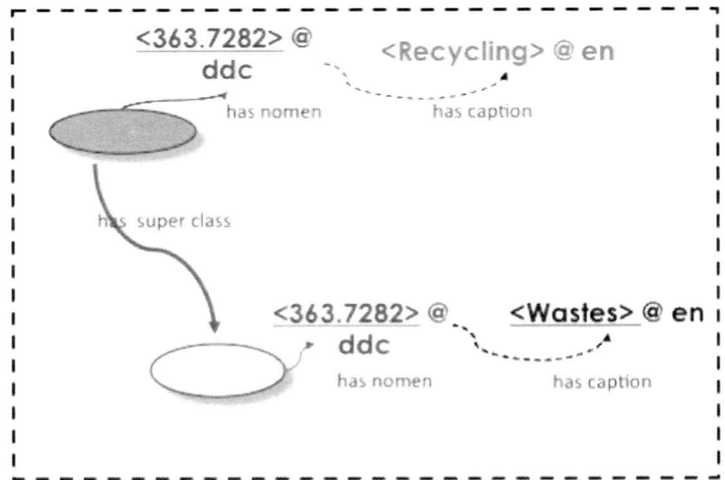

Thema-to-*Thema* Relationships Crosswalked through *Nomens* in Multiple Knowledge Organization Systems

This section provides examples of intersystem *thema* crosswalking through *nomens*.

Example: Cross-system Data between INSPEC Thesaurus *and* INSPEC Classification

```
Recycling
    BT    waste management
    TT    environmental factors; Management
    CC    B0170Q; B8699; E1840
```

Note: The example is from the *INSPEC Thesaurus* (2004 version; full record can be found on page 642). Here TT means "Top Term" (pointing to the top hierarchical concept) and CC means "Classification Code" of the *INSPEC Classification*.

The example demonstrates that a *thema* can be crosswalked through the *nomens* in two different authority systems, where <recycling> is a *nomen* (in a form of a thesaurus term) from the *INSPEC Thesaurus* and <B0170Q> is one of the *nomens* (in a form of a notation) from the *INSPEC Classification*. See Figure 7.14.

FIGURE 7.14   Illustration of the intersystem *themas'* crosswalking between *INSPEC Thesaurus* and *INSPEC Classification.*

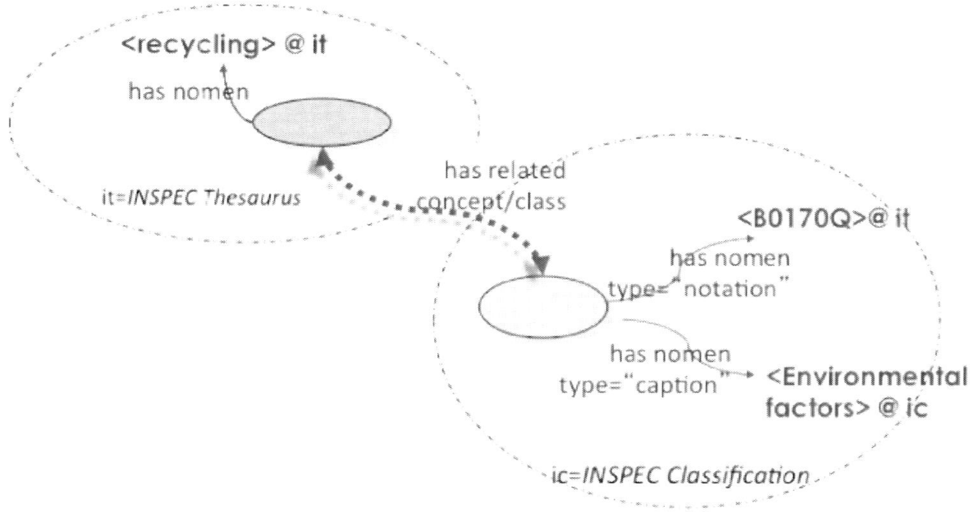

Example: Cross-system Data between LCSH and LCC

LC Control Number: sh85145542
     150 $a Water conservation
     053 _0 #a TD388 $b TD388.5

Note: The MARC21 coding used is:

150 = Heading—Topical term

053 = LC Classification Number

This same record is also used in a previous section "Example: Data Extracted from an LC Subject Authority Record—Genus-Species Relationship" when semantic relationships between *themas* from the same scheme are presented. Here it is the relationships of *themas* from different schemes that are further explored.

In this example, the *thema* represented by the *nomen* <water conservation> in LCSH is crosswalked to the LCC, where the *thema* is placed in a class <TD388.5> and a subclass <TD388.5>. Figure 7.15 illustrates such relationships.

FIGURE 7.15   Illustration of the intersystem *themas'* crosswalking between LCSH and LCC.

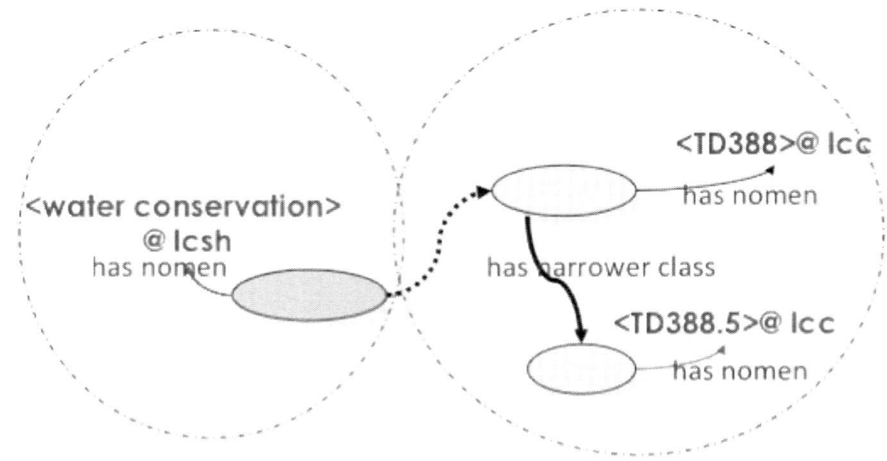

SAME *THEMA* REPRESENTED BY *NOMENS* FROM DIFFERENT SCHEMES

The following case demonstrates that, to some extent, the granularity of a *thema* is also dependent on its appellations in a particular scheme.

For example, a resource is about marriage customs in sixteenth-century France. The *thema* will be represented by the *nomens* established in different schemes, such as:

LCC: <GT2749.A2>

    Constructed/combined from:

    Manners and customs (General)

    –Customs relative to private life

    –Love. Courtship. Marriage. Sex customs—Marriage customs

    –By region or country

    –Europe

    GT2749—France

    .A2—General works

DDC: <392.50944>

    Constructed/combined from:

    Social sciences

    –Customs, etiquette & folklore

    –Customs

    –Customs of life cycle and domestic life

    392.5—Wedding and marriage customs

    -0944—France

LCSH:

    <Marriage customs and rites—France—History>

    <Marriage customs and rites—France—History—16th century>

FAST:

    <Marriage customs and rites—History>

    <France>

    <16th Century>

As this example demonstrates, schemes may allow the representation of *themas* at different levels of specificity through the structure and syntax of the *nomens* they have established.

REFERENCES

Art and Architecture Thesaurus (AAT). (2000–). Los Angeles: J. Paul Getty Trust, Vocabulary Program. Available at http://www.getty.edu/research/tools/vocabularies/aat/index.html (accessed April 19, 2012). Hierarchy Display, available at http://www.getty.edu/vow/AATHierarchy?find=&logic=AND¬e=&english=N&subjectid=300000000. About the AAT, available at http://www.getty.edu/research/tools/vocabularies/aat/about.html.

Faceted Application of Subject Terminology (FAST). (2001–). OCLC Online Computer Library Center. Available at http://www.oclc.org/research/activities/fast/default.htm (accessed April 19, 2012).

Foundational Model of Anatomy Ontology (FMA). 2006. School of Medicine, University of Washington. Available at http://sig.biostr.washington.edu/projects/fm/index.html (accessed July 25, 2011).

National Library of Medicine (NLM). (2003–). *Unified Medical Language System*. Homepage available at http://www.nlm.nih.gov/research/umls/ (accessed July 25, 2011).

National Library of Medicine (NLM). (2009) *UMLS Reference Manual*. Available at http://www.ncbi.nlm.nih.gov/books/NBK9676/ (accessed July 25, 2011). 5.4 Hierarchies for Semantic Types and Semantic Relations in the Semantic Network. Current Semantic Types, available at http://www.nlm.nih.gov/research/umls/META3_current_semantic_types.html.

CHAPTER 8

Use of FRSAD for Knowledge Organization Structure Development and Interoperability

FRSAD FOR KNOWLEDGE ORGANIZATION STRUCTURE DEVELOPMENT

One of the fundamental notions of the *thema-nomen* model for subject authority data is to separate *themas* from what they are known as, referred to, or addressed as. This fundamental notion is consistent with KOS' structures. Emphasizing this notion will help common understanding of KOS principles and the development of any KOS.

Implications of FRSAD for Various Knowledge Organization Structures

Implications of FRSAD can be discussed based on the structures of subject authority systems or types of KOS. The basic elements in any KOS can be analyzed from the FRSAD perspective regarding its

1. *Thema*
2. *Nomen*
3. Relationships:
   - *Thema*-to-*nomen*
   - *Thema*-to-*thema*
   - *Nomen*-to-*nomen*
4. Attributes of *thema*
5. Attributes of *nomen*

Themas in different KOS vocabularies could have different granularity; some are regarded as single concepts in contrast with complex concepts; represented by various appellations in single terms, compound terms, or multiple-word terms; and pre-coordinated or stand-alone. Table 8.1 attempts to list the high-level "*thema* hasAppellation *nomen*" relationship as commonly seen in various types of KOS vocabularies according to the conventional terminology used by respective communities. Also note that although in general the relationships between these two entities are many-to-many, controlled

TABLE 8.1 *Thema* and *nomen* in various KOS

KOS	Thema	Nomen
Thesauri	Concept	Terms (preferred and non-preferred)
Subject heading systems	Concept	Terms of pre-coordinated strings
Taxonomies	Category	Category labels (with or without notations)
Controlled lists	Concept or name	Terms
Classification systems	Class (in the context of the full category description of the class)	Notations

vocabularies should follow the requirement that a *nomen* is only one *thema*'s appellation, while a *thema* can have multiple *nomens* (refer to Section " 'Has Appellation' Relationship") in one system.

Thesauri usually comply with international standards such as ISO 2788 and ISO 5964. Subject heading schemes such as the LCSH have also adopted the basic structure of the thesaurus for the last two decades. Classification systems have implemented different practices and are usually constructed according to specific conventions and examples. In a typical enumerative (or enumerative-based) classification, each class corresponds to a *thema*, and a notation associated with the class is the *nomen*. Because of the comprehensive content and notes included in a class description, the *thema* is represented by the full description of the class. *Nomen* is the symbol (or surrogate) used to represent a *thema* such as the notation, full caption, and the URI of the class when the classification is published as Linked Data.

In comparison with thesaurus structure, relationships between *themas* and *nomens* and their major attributes in a typical classification system may demonstrate the need for further study (Table 8.2).

It is obvious that FRSAD would work very well with structures used in simple controlled lists, thesauri, and subject heading lists. For taxonomies and classifications, there might exist a need to have case-by-case analysis in order to align the elements designed by FRSAD to their macro-structures that inherit certain conventions.

FRSAD for Authority Data in General

The contribution of FRSAD to the bibliographic universe and beyond is its applicability for both subject and non-subject authority data that are used for expressing either aboutness or ofness of intellectual and artistic works. In the library community, a name authority for the responsible bodies is usually a

TABLE 8.2 Common relationships between *themas* and *nomens*, major attributes of *thema* and of *nomen* in thesauri and classification systems

	Thema-to-*Thema* Relations	*Thema* Attributes	*Nomen*-to-*Nomen* Relations	*Nomen* Attributes
Thesauri	• hierarchical . broader . narrower • associative . related	• scope note • concept type	• preferred and non-preferred terms	• type • language • [administrative] • audience • time of validity . . .
Classification systems	• hierarchical . subclass . built class • polyhierarchical • member inclusive • member exclusive • associative	• note • class type	• notation and full caption • caption and caption	• type • language • [administrative] . . .

separate structure from a thesaurus or subject heading authority file. However, it is not rare to see a KOS (e.g., a thesaurus) be used for managing the data about agents, such as people or corporate bodies. Good examples include the Getty's *Union List of Artist Names* (ULAN) and the *Virtual International Authority File* (VIAF).

ULAN was originally constructed as a simple alphabetized "union list" of clustered artist names and biographies, part of the Getty's effort in 1984 of merging and coordinating controlled vocabulary resources for use by the automated documentation projects of the J. Paul Getty Trust. "[I]n the late 1990s ULAN was brought into compliance with national and international standards for thesaurus construction. Its scope was broadened to include corporate bodies such as architectural firms and repositories of art, which may have hierarchical levels" ("About the ULAN," updated July 2007.). ULAN's international reputation has proven its success, including both the content covered and the delivery of the content using the thesaurus structure.

VIAF is a gateway to access millions of name authority records and their associated bibliographic metadata provided by a great number of national libraries in the world (VIAF, 2010–). VIAF is modeling the agents including persons and corporate bodies. For example, each person has a unique identifier; all authority data about this person, regardless of the name by which the person may be recorded in various authority schemes, are presented together. Considering this person as a thing, the *thema* is this conceptualized person, and the *nomens* are all constructed headings of the person's names. The difference of VIAF from other name authorities is that it is a hub of approximately 20 authority schemes rather than being a single authority file. Also, in an authority cluster (a record view) for an agent, no preferred *nomen* to a *thema* is selected. (See Figure 8.1, where three forms of constructed headings of "Jeanne-Claude" are corresponding to this artist instead of one preferred form.)

Taking the environmental artist Jeanne-Claude as an example, the aggregated data include all entries of Jeanne-Claude (with an ID 79151260) from various name authority schemes. The authority cluster provides her name appearing in name authorities or bibliographic records using various conventions, with the dates of her birth and death and without. In this example, as of March 27, 2011, seven preferred forms and 48 alternative names from individual authority files are recorded (some are identical) (Figure 8.1).

FIGURE 8.1   Preferred and alternative forms of Jeanne-Claude in VIAF. (VIAF, http://viaf.org/viaf/79151260/#Jeanne-Claude,_1935-2009. Reprinted with permission.)

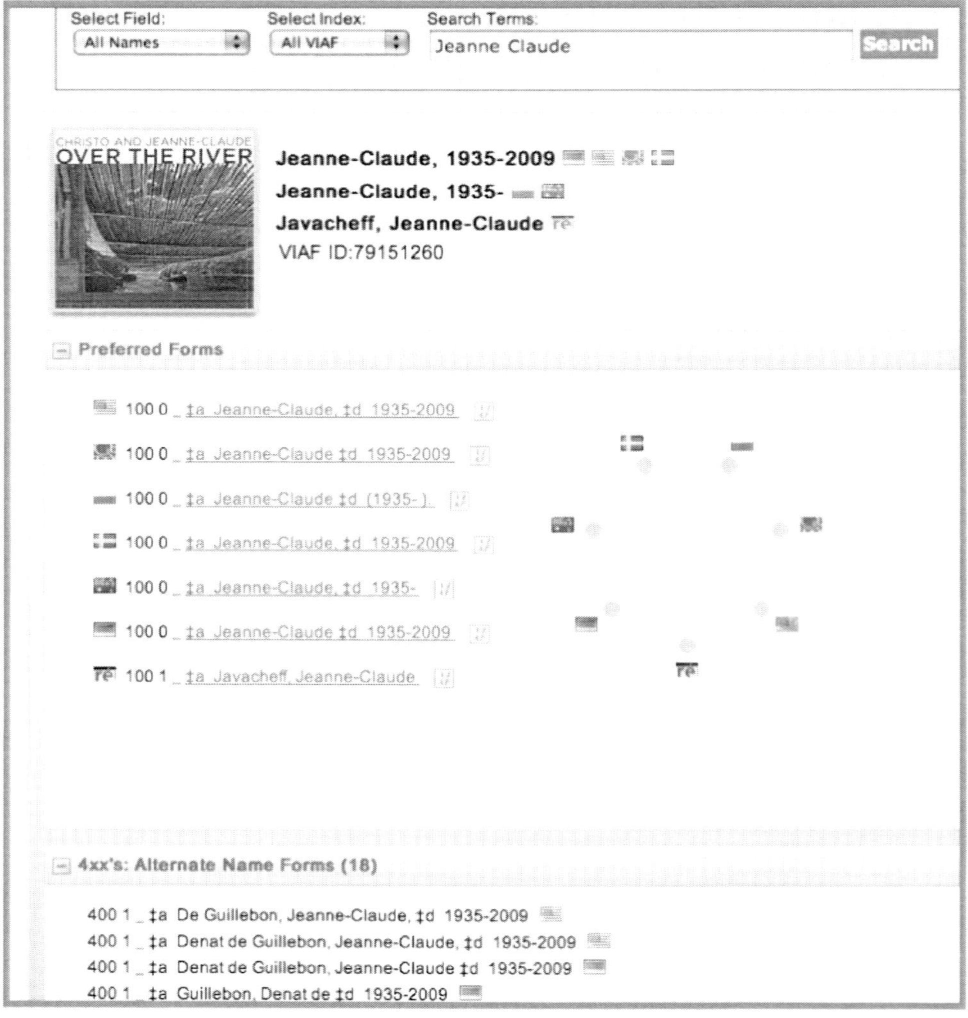

In other words, all *nomens* chosen to be preferred by involved schemes, plus the alternative forms recorded in each particular scheme, are provided according to the same *thema*.

The way the disambiguation and synonym controls ensured by VIAF work is to use the attributes of a *nomen* fully, as explained by Hickey (2009): "With many millions of names, even fairly uncommon names can represent multiple people, and we do our best to link people across files without making links we are not quite sure about. To make a link we need to have matching birth and death years, or other supporting information such as a title or co-author in common or sometimes a combination of partial matches on several different fields. The enriched VIAF records created as the result of all this matching bring together more information than exists in any single authority record" (Hickey, 2009, http://www.oclc.org/us/en/nextspace/013/research .htm).

Let's also take a look at the RDF/XML record of Jeanne-Claude in VIAF (http://viaf.org/viaf/79151260/rdf.xml). The cluster of name authority data from various files are all put into one "bucket," which has a unique identifier and is an RDF resource (or "thing") (<viaf:NameAuthorityCluster rdf:about="viaf/79151260">). Each name authority entry, for instance the data from the Library of Congress Name Authority, contains its local ID for the agent, the scheme's identifier, and preferred and alternative labels. All of these are encoded in VIAF with classes and properties defined by SKOS and SKOS Extension for Labels (SKOS-XL). (More about SKOS and SKOS-XL can be found in Section "The FRSAD Conceptual Model and Its Implementation in Data Models for Subject Authority Data"). For the bucket itself, VIAF ontology 1.1 defined a "hasEstablishedForm" property. It should be noted that in the FRSAD model, "established form" is recommended as a typical value for the *nomen* "type" attribute.

The most recent development of the Metadata Authority Description Schema (MADS) echoes the idea that all authority data (subject or not) can be modeled the same way. In MADS ontology's RDF version, a madsrdf:Authority is defined as a subclass of skos:Concept (MADS/RDF Documentation, 2011). An "Authority" (or "Authoritative form") is a concept (resource) with a controlled label; a "Label" is the lexical string that is the primary focus of an Authority, Variant, or Deprecated-authority description.

There could be more examples of how the FRSAD model would be appropriate for other kinds of resources. The current discussion only demonstrates the applicability of FRSAD to any kind of authority data. FRSAD's modeling of *nomen* as an entity allows tremendous flexibility for modeling attributes and attribute values for *nomens* representing *themas*.

FRSAD FOR MEETING MULTILINGUAL AND MULTIPLE COMMUNITY NEEDS

The potential of FRSAD for multilingual efforts deserves to be emphasized, too. In a world that is more closely connected in almost all aspects, a symmetrical multilingual thesaurus, or a multiple-accessible index to a vocabulary, can be characterized as *nomen*-oriented efforts. In another word, their focus is on using different *nomens* for the same concept. Semantic relationships are not changed because of the vocabulary's being in a different language environment.

A multilingual controlled vocabulary can be generated in the process of building a new vocabulary or translating an existing source controlled vocabulary into a target. The FRSAD model will help the process through its fundamental notion of separating *themas* from what they are known as, referred to, or addressed as. In a symmetrical multilingual vocabulary development, the key is to respect the original semantics of the concepts, including their definitions and scope notes and the semantic relationships between and among concepts. The following attributes defined for *nomens* can assist in the establishment and management of multilingual appellations for a *thema*.

- **Language of *nomen*** (Examples of attribute values: Greek, Arabic)
- **Script of *nomen*** (Examples of values: Chinese (Simplified), Chinese (Traditional))
- **Script conversion** (Examples of values: ISO 3602, 1998, Romanization of Japanese [kana script])
- **Audience** (Examples of values: Spanish-speaking users, Scientists, Children)

In the international standard (ISO, 2011) and best practices, sublanguages (e.g., American English, British English, and Indian English) may be treated as different languages. Similarly, the terminology preferred by different communities (e.g., scientists) or targeted audiences (e.g., children) can be treated as different languages. Websites that have audiences of both scientists and non-scientists, such as the World Wildlife Fund (http://gis.wwfus.org/wildfinder/) and Ocean Biogeographic Information System (OBIS) (www.iobis.org/) always allow searching of the same data with common names and scientific names and display the names side by side. The attributes listed above also serve the needs in these use cases.

FRSAD MODEL FOR VOCABULARY MAPPING

The FRSAD model can be applied to vocabulary mapping according to different needs. Two approaches for two different situations are illustrated in this section.

FIGURE 8.2 Illustration of a *nomen*-hosting system where *nomens* are attributes of a *thema*.

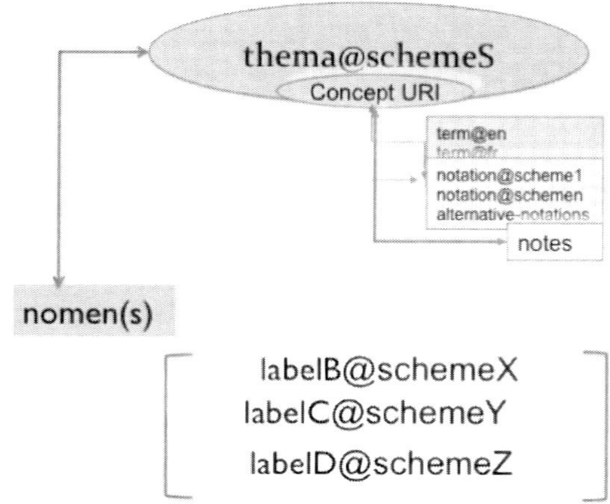

Approach 1: *Nomen*-hosting System

This applies to the situation when a FRSAD-ified vocabulary system (i.e., one that has implemented the *thema-nomen* model) needs to map to other vocabularies that have not implemented the model. A significant difference can be found between these vocabularies, where *nomens* are only attributes of a *thema*. If *nomens* are attributes, they cannot possess any attributes of their own, and the management of the *nomens* and *themas* is mixed.

If we consider the FRSAD-ified vocabulary as the source scheme (scheme S), each *thema* in scheme S will host all *nomens* representing *themas* that are mapped (Figure 8.2).

The advantage of such an approach is that while other systems have not implemented the *thema-nomen* model, the FRSAD-ified system can still record mapped results. There are two disadvantages of such an approach: (1) any change in a target vocabulary will have to be reflected in this hosting system; (2) any *nomen* from another target vocabulary does not have attributes to indicate its status, time of validity, and so forth unless the hosting system wants to manage them.

Approach 2: *Thema*-centered System

The second situation is ideal where each vocabulary involved in the mapping has already implemented the FRSAD model. In such a case, each *thema* of a source scheme (scheme S) is mapped from individual *themas* (including built and postcoordinated) from other target sources. Any *thema* retains its own semantic relations between and among *themas* and between *thema* and *nomens*. Each *nomen* has its own attributes as well. All are retained after the mapping. Using the properties defined by SKOS, the degree of matching between each pair can be indicated (Figure 8.3).

FIGURE 8.3   Illustration of a *thema*-centered system where each vocabulary has already implemented the FRSAD model.

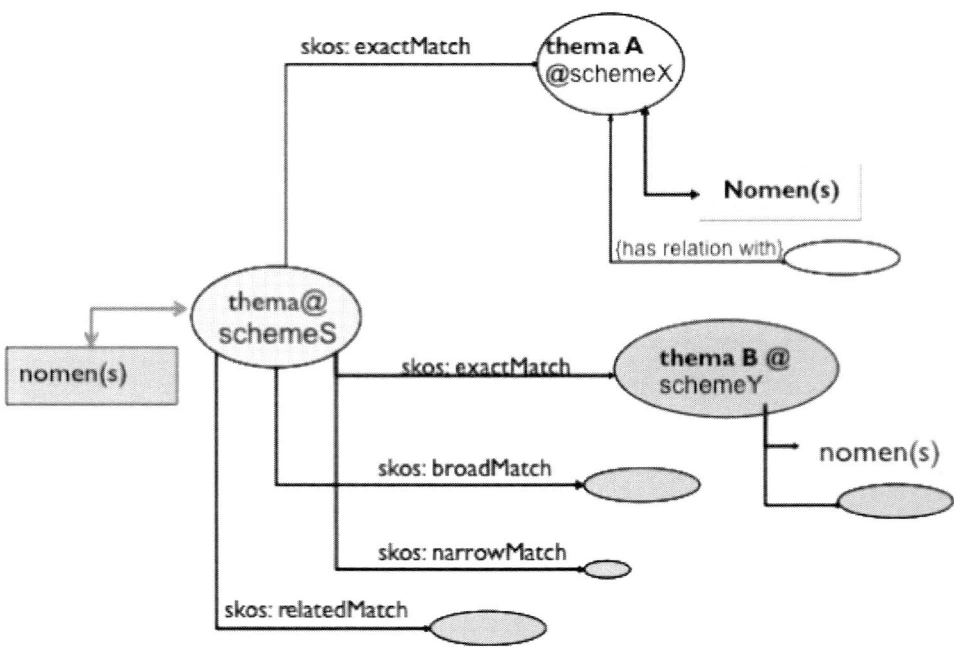

The advantages are inherited from the FRSAD model, where *nomens* can be changed or added easily (e.g., another language version for a multilingual thesaurus or a translated classification). New KOS vocabularies can be included continuously. The contingency is that target systems need to have implemented the FRSAD model to manage their *themas* and *nomens*.

THE FRSAD CONCEPTUAL MODEL AND ITS IMPLEMENTATION IN DATA MODELS FOR SUBJECT AUTHORITY DATA

In the last decades, KOS, including especially thesauri, classification schemes, and lists of subject headings, have mainly followed or conformed with the established data models defined by standards, recommendations, or best practices. The long list contains some standards that are widely used, such as ISO 5964, ISO 2788, NISO Z39.19, IFLA Principles Underlying Subject Heading Languages, and MARC21 Format for Classification Data.

The FRSAD conceptual model was an attempt to construct a general conceptual model above all these data models, with the purpose of assisting in an assessment of the potential for international sharing and use of subject authority data both within the library sector and beyond.

The FRSAD model, especially the second segment, the *thema-nomen* relationship, is important in two aspects.

SKOS and the *Thema-Nomen* Relationship Model

The first importance of the *thema-nomen* model is the conceptualization of the relationship between a concept (*thema*) and the representation(s) of the concept (*nomen*(s)). This conceptualization can be found to have echoes in the SKOS Core (SKOS Core Vocabulary Specification, 2005) draft data model back in 2005 when the FRSAR Working Group started.

The SKOS Core model clearly emphasizes a concept-centric view of vocabulary, where primitive objects are not labels; rather, they are concepts represented by labels. The root of the model can be found in the thesaurus standards developed before SKOS Core, but such an emphasis was not clearly stated or modeled due to the mix of relationships of concepts (e.g., BT, NT, and RT) and between the concept and its labels (Use and Used For [UF]). The use of the word *term* in semantic relationships of broader and narrower concepts reflects such a mixed representation. In the SKOS Core model, labels (preferred, alternative, and hidden) are affiliates of a concept while the semantic relationships exist among concepts. "Mirroring the fundamental categories of relations that are used in vocabularies such as thesauri [ISO2788], SKOS supplies three standard properties" (SKOS Primer, 2009) for semantic relationships: skos:broader and skos:narrower for hierarchical links and skos: related for associative (non-hierarchical) links. These convey the same relationships between *themas* defined in the FRSAD model.

Figure 8.4 presents a typical thesaurus entry to the corresponding SKOS attributes.

FIGURE 8.4   SKOS for a typical thesaurus entry.

Note: labels are attribute/surrogates of a concept.

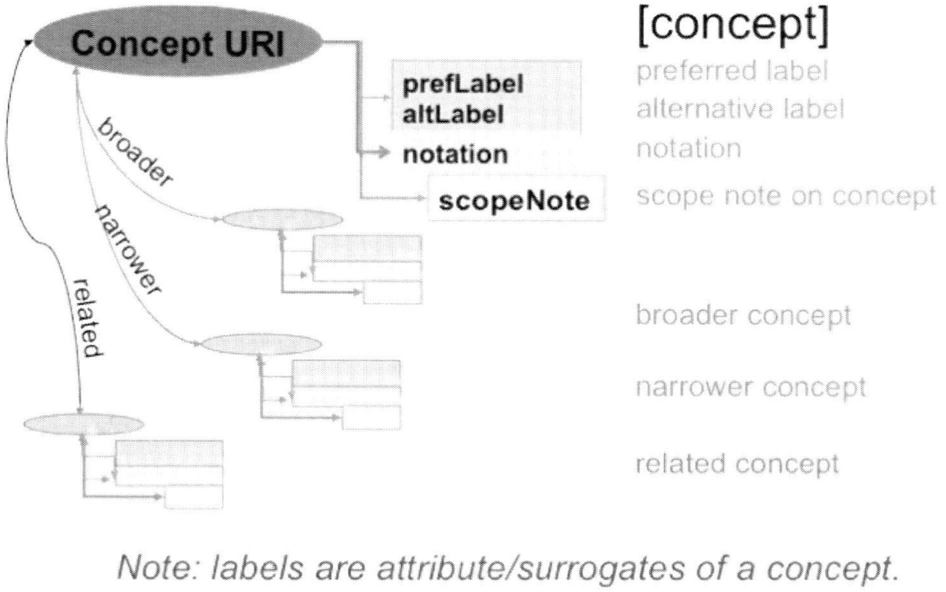

The KOS vocabularies that have implemented this SKOS core (or no extension for labels) model can be found in those already published as Linked Data, such as the early version of LCSH at http://id.loc.gov/authorities/subjects.html (LCSH Linked Data version 2009–).

SKOS eXtension for Labels (SKOS-XL) and Relationships of *Nomens*

The FRSAD model has another significance, which is the addition of an entity, *nomen*, to the original proposed FRBR. This enables the treatment of the so-called label class to be an entity itself, which in turn allows systems to define attributes of this entity as well as relationships between instances of a *nomen*.

This aspect is parallel with the newer and official W3C Recommendation version of the SKOS (2009), which supplements an eXtension for Labels (SKOS-XL) specification that defines an extension, providing additional support for identifying, describing and linking lexical entities. To align with the SKOS 2009 specification, *thema* would correspond to skos:Concept class and *nomen* will correspond to skosxl:Label class, as illustrated in Figure 8.5.

The FRSAD model defines *nomen* as an entity; therefore, *nomens* can have attributes as well as relations between or among themselves while representing the same concept. This can be explained with a situation when a preferred label of a concept in a concept scheme has various literal forms, synonyms, statuses of release, and administrated data. FRSAD has provided a few common possible relationships and allows new relationships to be added in implementations. With SKOS-XL becoming available, such situations can be handled appropriately.

FIGURE 8.5   Aligning FRSAD model with SKOS + SKOS-XL data model; the capitalization of "Concept" and "Label" means that they are classes.

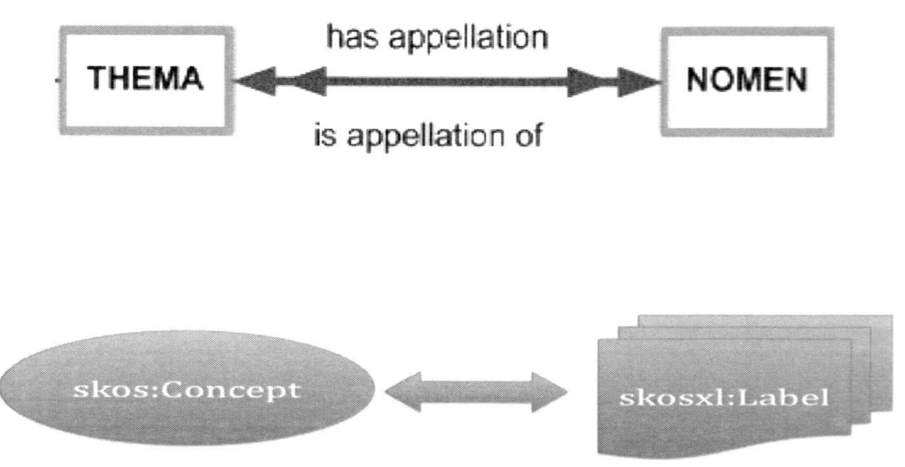

FIGURE 8.6   Simplified illustration of a multilingual thesaurus entry data model where "Label" is an entity and has attributes.

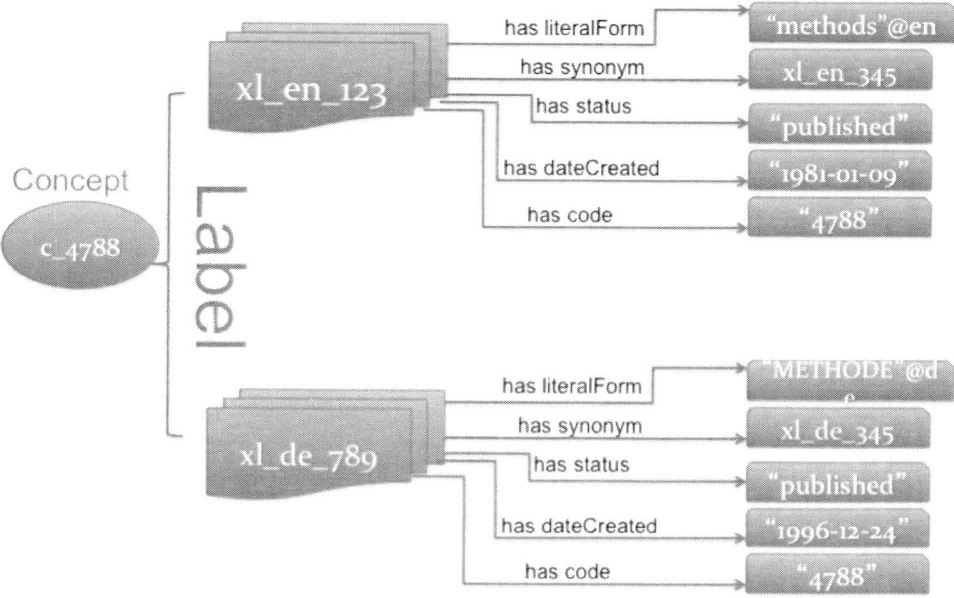

Taking an example of a multilingual thesaurus entry from AGROVOC, both the concept and label classes clearly stand as separate entities (AGROVOC Linked Data version, 2011-). Each preferred label has its literal form, synonym, status, creation date, and other administrative information. If multiple languages are involved, this model will be further extended (Figure 8.6).

1. Each concept has multiple preferred labels with different languages. (Each language has one preferred label.)

2. Each concept also has one or more non-preferred labels of each language involved. They are considered as synonyms of the preferred label.

3. Multilingual preferred labels have different literal forms, synonyms, status, creation date, and other administrative information.

It should be noted that the labels have attributes, such as "has literalForm," "has synonym," and "has status." These would correspond to FRSAD *nomen* attributes.

It should also be noted that each label (preferred or synonym) has been assigned a unique identifier. In the figure, short IDs are used to replace the real HTTP (Hypertext Transfer Protocol) URIs representing the concept and labels. For example, "http://aims.fao.org/aos/agrovoc/c_4788" is shortened as "c_4788" in the figure. Further explanations include:

- "c_4788" represents a concept instance.
- "xl_en_123" represents the English preferred label of concept "c_4788."

- "xl_de_789" represents the German preferred label of the same concept.
- "xl_en_345" is a synonym of the preferred label "xl_en_123."

Back to SKOS, all original functions for the "Concept" class still apply (e.g., for presenting the established semantic relationships between concepts, the attributes of concepts, and for organizing concepts in a concept schema, aggregating, and mapping concepts from different schemas), and these are also applied to the SKOS-XL "Label" class.

While the most common relationships and attributes are specified in FRSAD, it is made clear that the list is not prescriptive: additional implementation- or domain-specific relationships and attributes can be added when needed. The two data models presented above demonstrate how the FRSAD model can be implemented as well as the power such a model wields to meet the needs of both the conventional LIS environment and the emerging Linked Data environment.

REFERENCES

About the ULAN. (Revised July 2011). The Getty Vocabulary Program, The J. Paul Getty Trust. Available at http://www.getty.edu/research/tools/vocabularies/ulan/about.html (accessed July 21, 2011).

AGROVOC Thesaurus (linked data version). (2011–). Food and Agriculture Organization of the United Nations. Retrieved from http://aims.fao.org/website/Linked-Open-Data/sub (accessed July 21, 2011).

Hickey, Thomas. (2009). "Expanding the Concept of Universal Bibliographic Control." *Next Space:The OCLC Newsletter*13 (September 2009), http://www.oclc.org/us/en/nextspace/013/research.htm (accessed July 21, 2011).

ISO. (2011). *ISO/CD 25964-1, Information and Documentation—Thesauri and Interoperability with Other Vocabularies—Part 1: Thesauri for Information Retrieval.* ISO/TC 46 / SC 9 ISO 25964 Working Group.

Library of Congress Subject Headings (linked data version). (2009–). Library of Congress. Available at http://id.loc.gov/authorities/subjects.html (accessed April 19, 2012).

MADS/RDF Documentation. (2011). Available from MADS official website at http://www.loc.gov/standards/mads/rdf/ (accessed April 19, 2012).

SKOS Core Vocabulary Specification. (2005). Eds. Miles, A. and Bechhofer, S. W3C Working Draft, May 10, 2005. Retrieved from http://www.w3.org/TR/2005/WD-swbp-skos-core-spec-20050510/ (accessed July 21, 2011).

"SKOS eXtension for Labels" (SKOS-XL). (2009). In *SKOS Simple Knowledge Organization System Reference*, edited by A. Miles and S. Bechhofer. W3C Recommendation. Appendix B. Retrieved from http://www.w3.org/TR/skos-reference/#xl (accessed April 19, 2012).

SKOS Simple Knowledge Organization System Primer. (2009). Edited by A. Isaac and E. Summers. W3C Working Group Note, August 18, 2009. Available at http://www.w3.org/TR/skos-primer/ (accessed July 21, 2011).

SKOS Simple Knowledge Organization System Reference (2009). Edited by A. Miles and S. Bechhofer. W3C Recommendation, August 18, 2009. Available at http://www.w3.org/TR/skos-reference/ (accessed July 21, 2011).

Union List of Artist Names (ULAN). (2010). J. Paul Getty Trust. Online version available at http://www.getty.edu/research/tools/vocabularies/ulan/index.html (accessed July 21, 2011).

VIAF. (2010–). Available at http://viaf.org/ (accessed July 21, 2011).

CHAPTER 9

Concluding Remarks

Providing subject access to resources was already specified by Cutter in 1876 (Cutter, 1904) as one of the objectives of a catalog:

1. to enable a person to find a book of which either
   - the author
   - the title
   - **the subject**

   is known.
2. to show what the library has
   - by a given author
   - **on a given subject**
   - in a given kind of literature
3. to assist in the choice of a book
   - as to its edition (bibliographically)
   - as to its character (literary or topical)

Many authors have written about the importance of subject access, and research has confirmed that while end users need to be able to search on a topic, they also find current catalogs and other bibliographic information systems difficult to use, particularly for subject searching.

After FRBR, the conceptual model of the bibliographic universe, was developed and accepted, it was time to focus on the "has as subject" relationship and develop that part of the model further. The IFLA FRSAR Working Group developed the conceptual model, FRSAD, within the FRBR framework, focusing on the aboutness of *works*. FRSAD's development started with user tasks, which ensured a structured frame of reference for relating the data that are recorded in subject authority records to the needs of the users of these data. The FRSAD model was also developed in the context of international sharing and use of subject authority data both within the library environment and beyond. For that reason the model is very general and at a level that is independent of any implementation, domain, system, or specific context.

The main advantage of the FRSAD model is that it enables focusing on the topic (concept) separately from the appellation(s) used for that concept. This approach is similar to the developments in the area of the Semantic Web, such as SKOS. FRSAD is applicable to all kinds of KOS, including not only the more widely used subject heading lists and related authority data but also more sophisticated KOS types such as thesauri, classification systems, and vocabulary mappings, to name a few. Developed as a more general model, it is also applicable to nonsubject authority data, such as authority files for agents, geographic names, terms, or codes, all of which mainly focus on the entity *nomen*.

In this book, FRSAD is presented in the context of the FRBR family of models; however, it is explained in a much broader context, and therefore a detailed knowledge of FRBR is not a prerequisite. Numerous examples illustrate the theoretical foundation of the model and should encourage its use in full implementations both in the libraries and further in the emerging Linked Data environment.

REFERENCE

Cutter, C. A. (1904). *Rules for a Dictionary Catalog*, 4th ed. Washington, DC: Government Printing Office.

Index

About the Authors

MAJA ŽUMER is professor in the Department of Library and Information Science and Book Studies at the University of Ljubljana, Slovenia. Žumer chaired the IFLA Working Group on Guidelines for National Bibliographies in the Digital Age and cochaired the IFLA Working Group on the Functional Requirements for Subject Authority Records (FRSAR), while also serving as a working group member in developing the IFLA Guidelines for Subject Access to National Bibliographies and as member of Functional Requirements for Bibliographic Records (FRBR) Review Group.

MARCIA LEI ZENG is professor in the School of Library and Information Science at Kent State University in Kent, OH. She chaired the IFLA Working Group on the Functional Requirements for Subject Authority Records (FRSAR) while also serving as a working group member in developing the IFLA Guidelines of Digital Libraries.

ATHENA SALABA is associate professor at the School of Library and Information Science, Kent State University, in Kent, OH. She cochaired the IFLA Working Group on the Functional Requirements for Subject Authority Records (FRSAR).